Temple of a Space Kitten

Unusual Watercolour Portraits

TRACY SHEPHERD

Find me on Youtbe: Mermaid in the Sea Tarot
Find me on Tiktok: TracyShepherdAuthor

ISBN 978-0-9959579-3-0

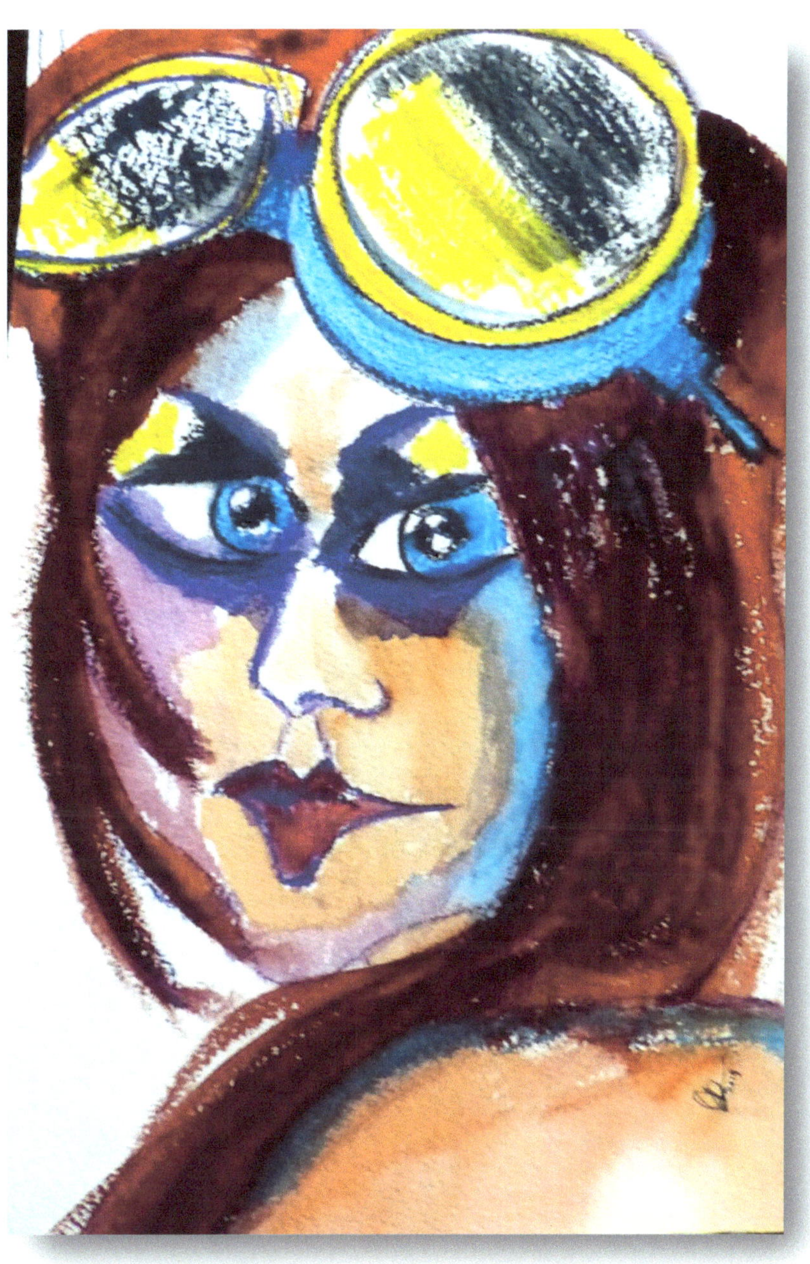

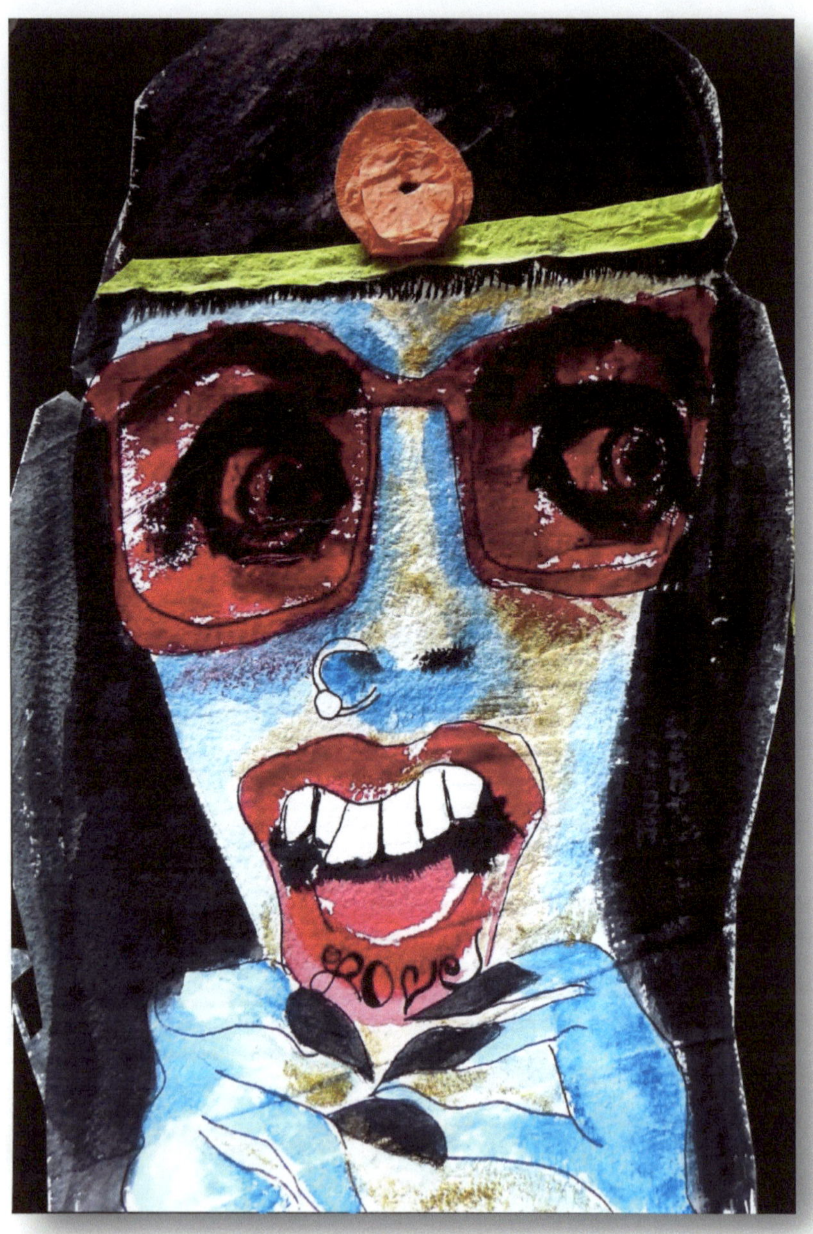
Love

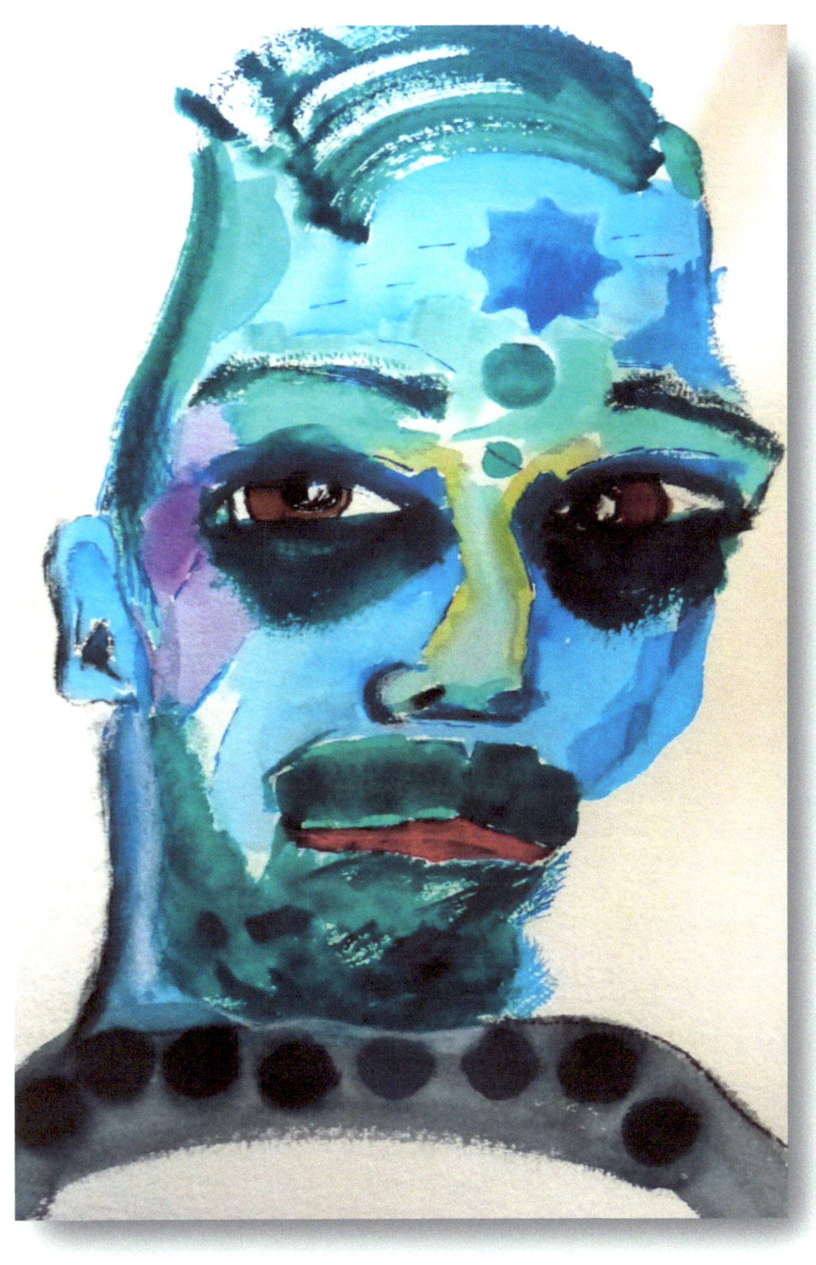

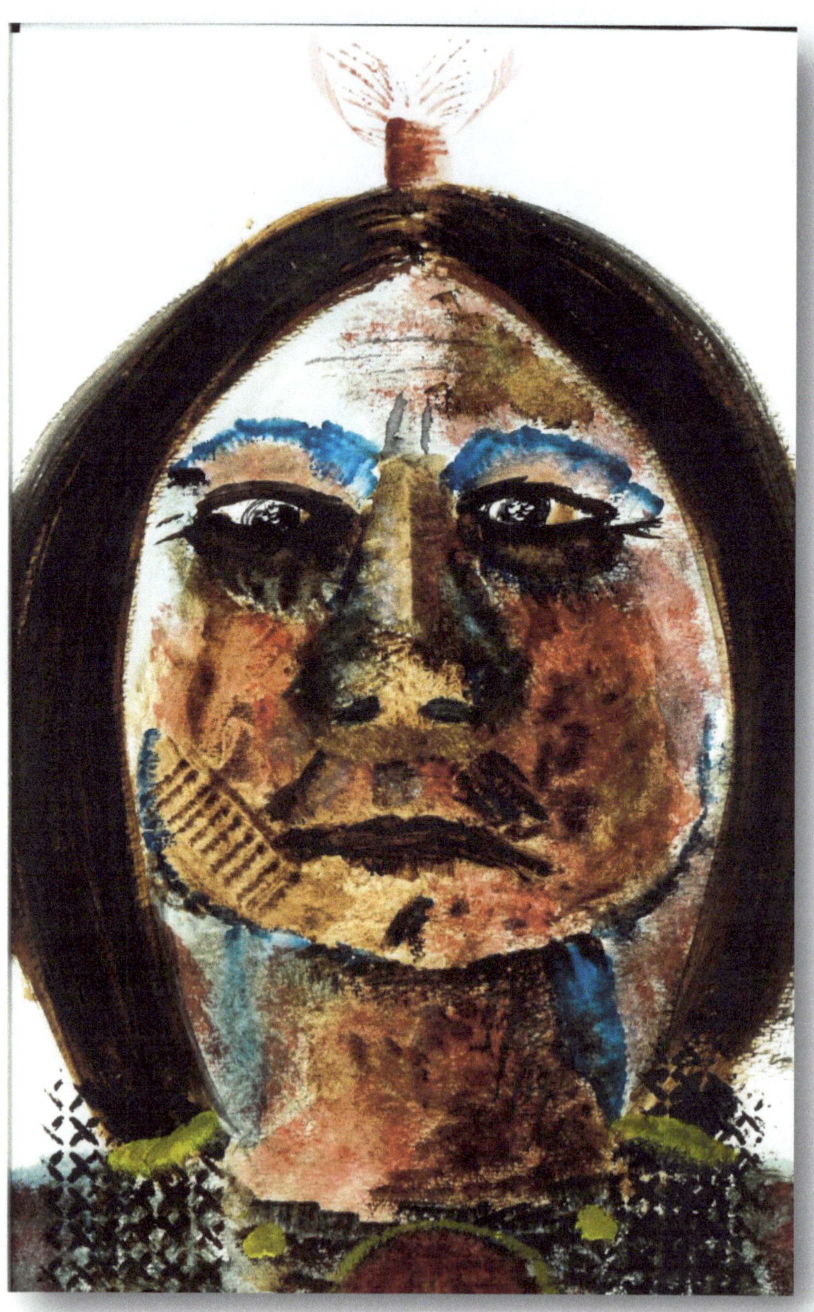

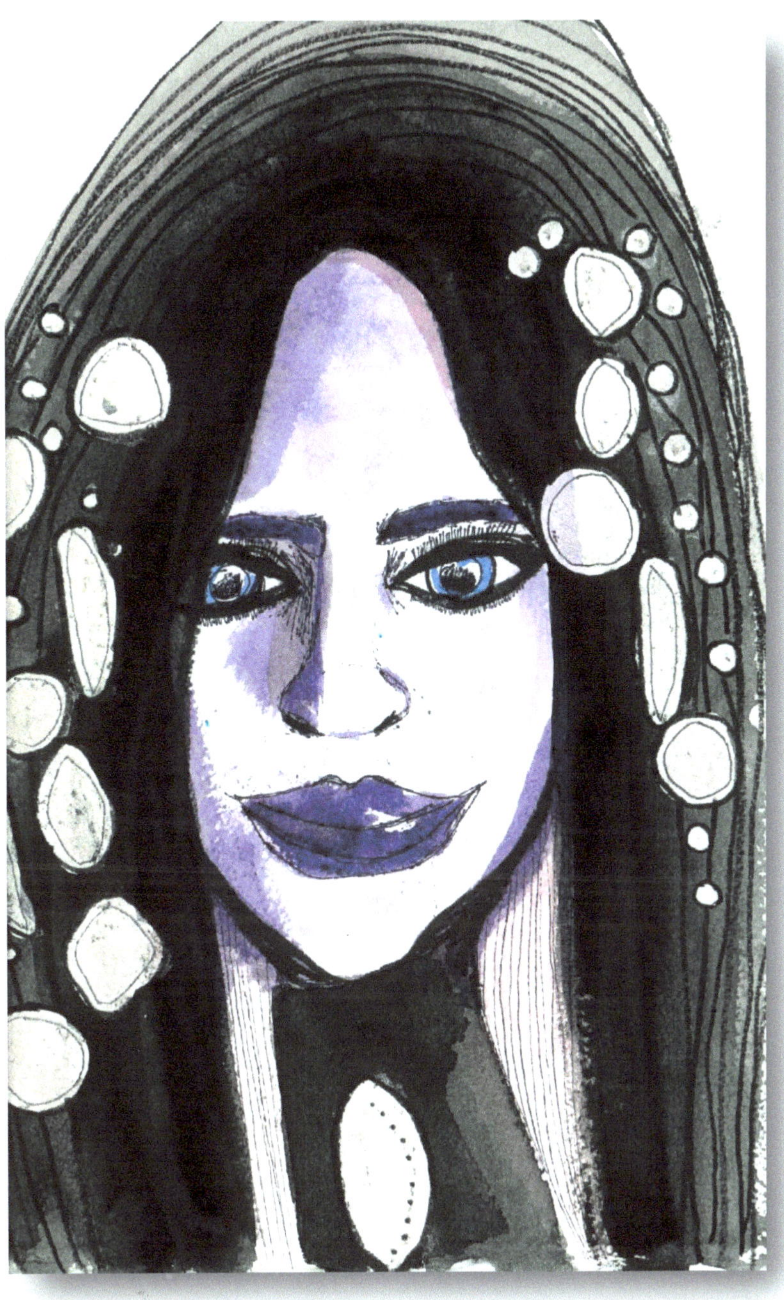

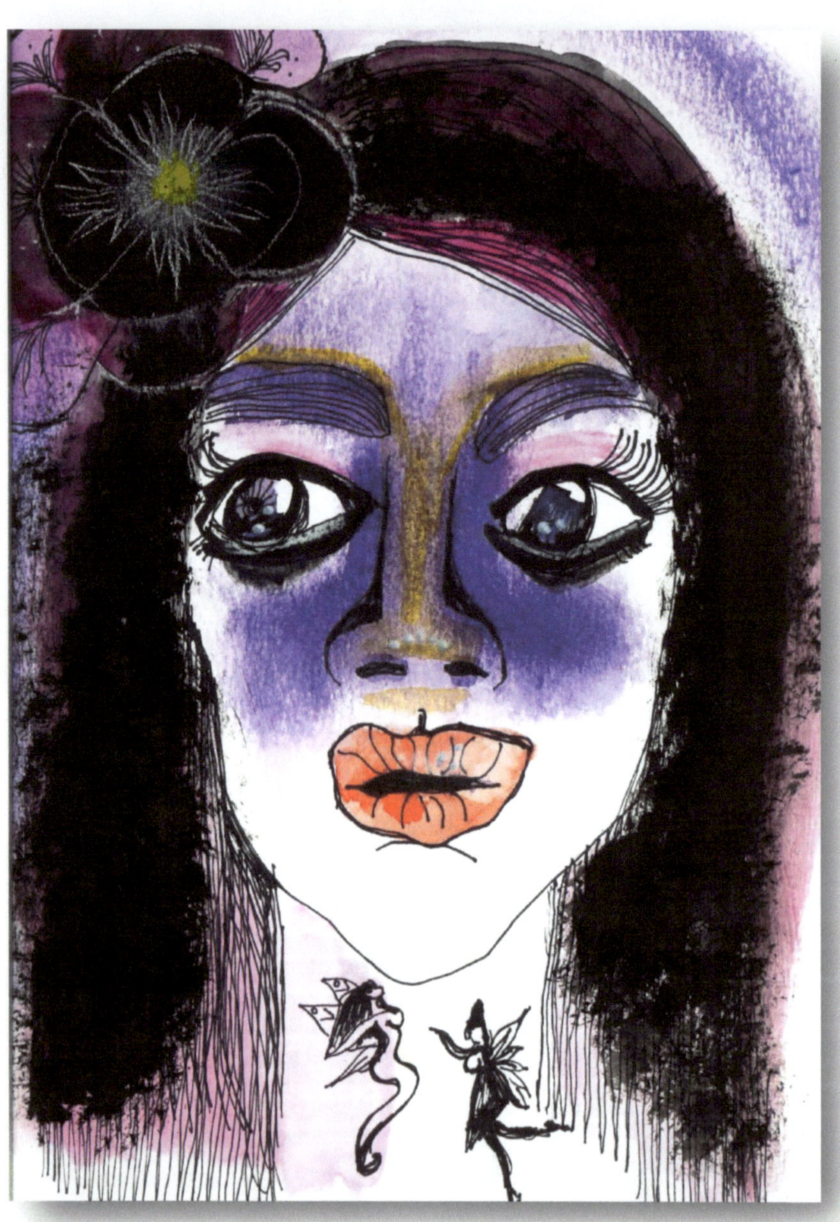

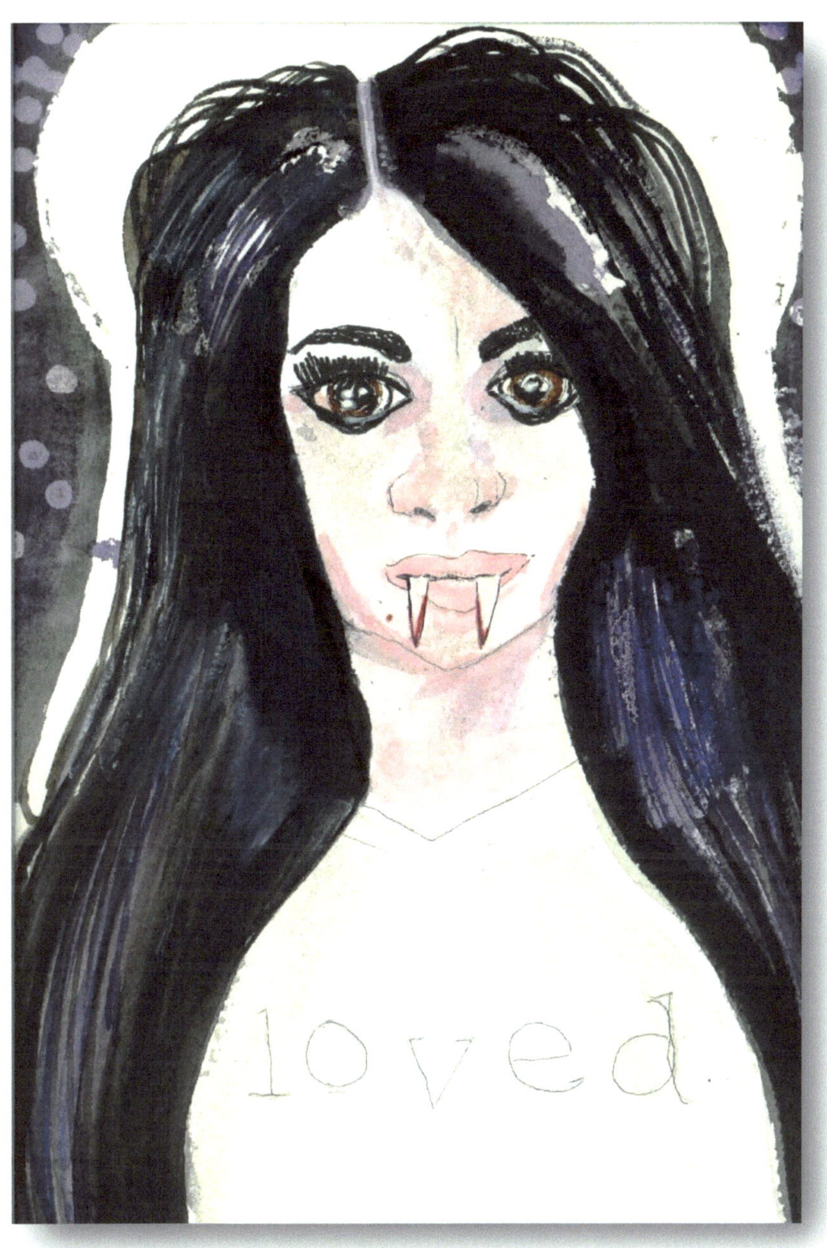
loved.

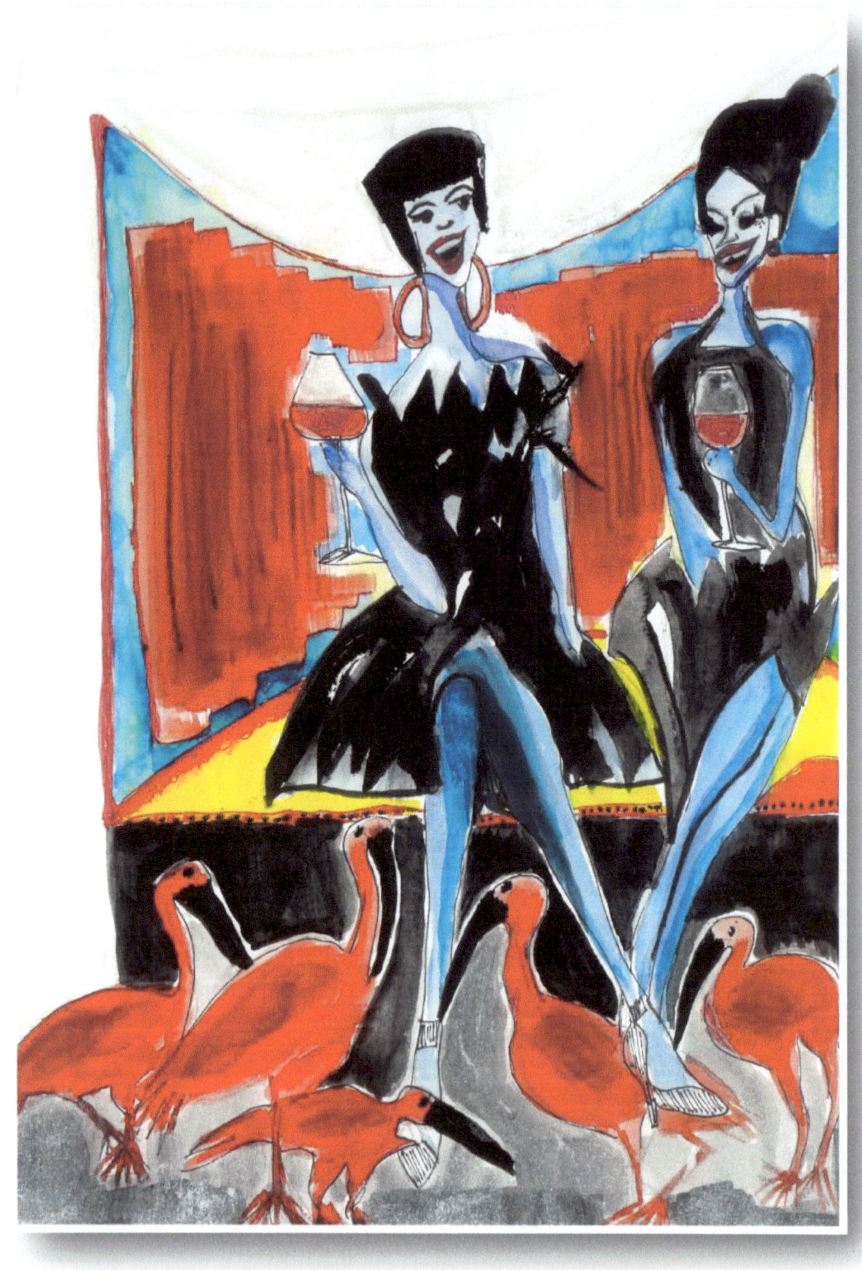

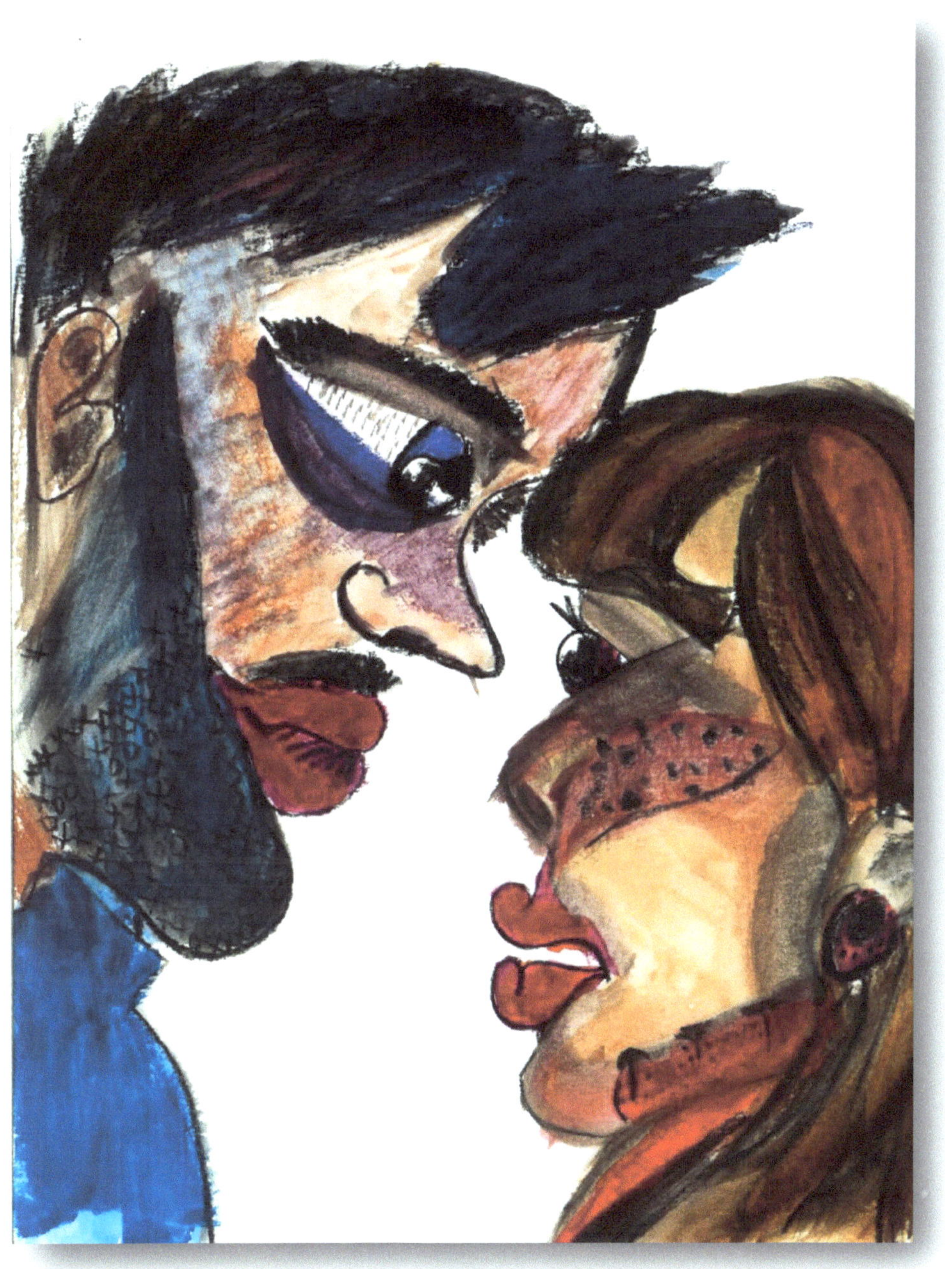

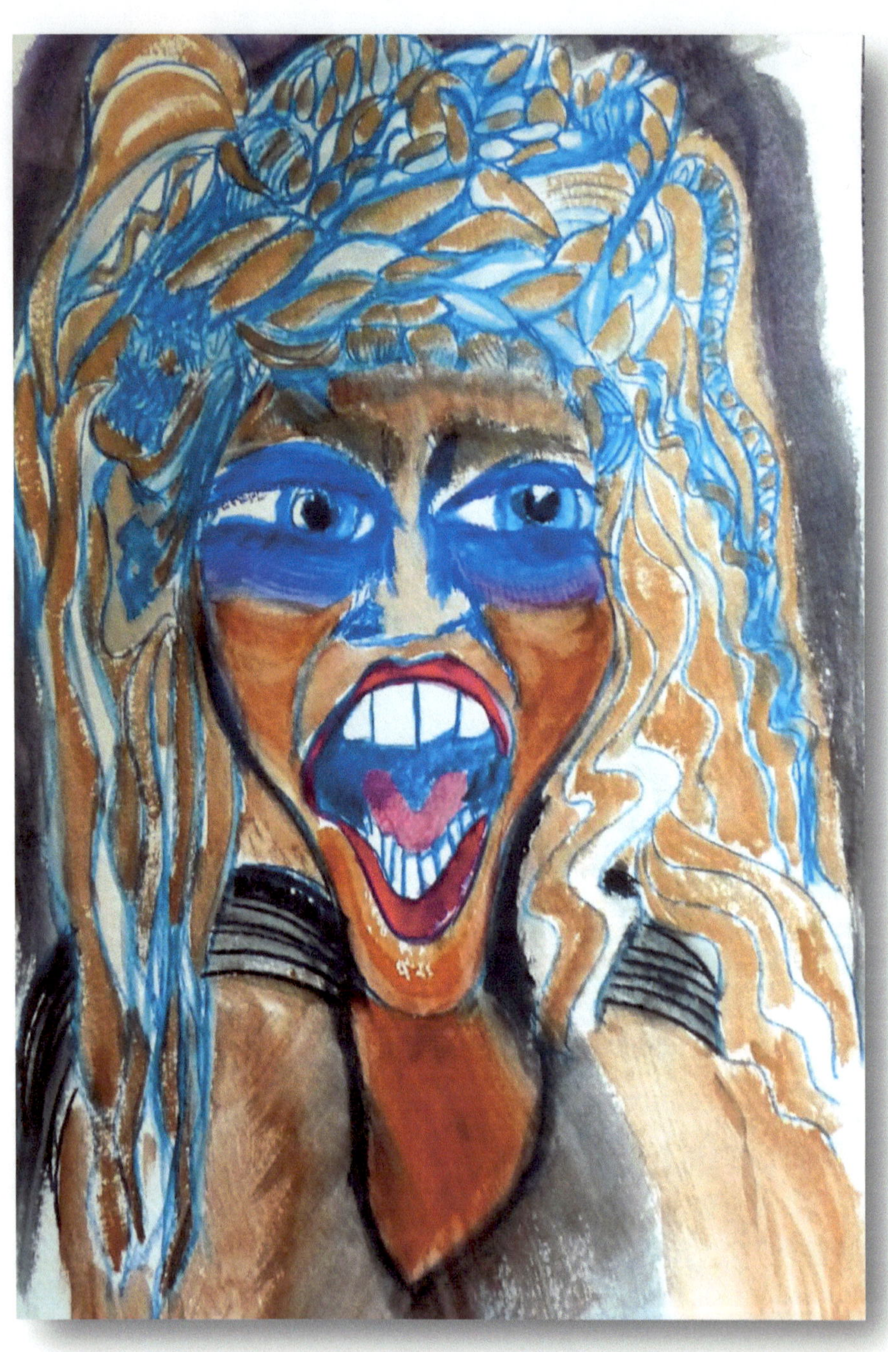

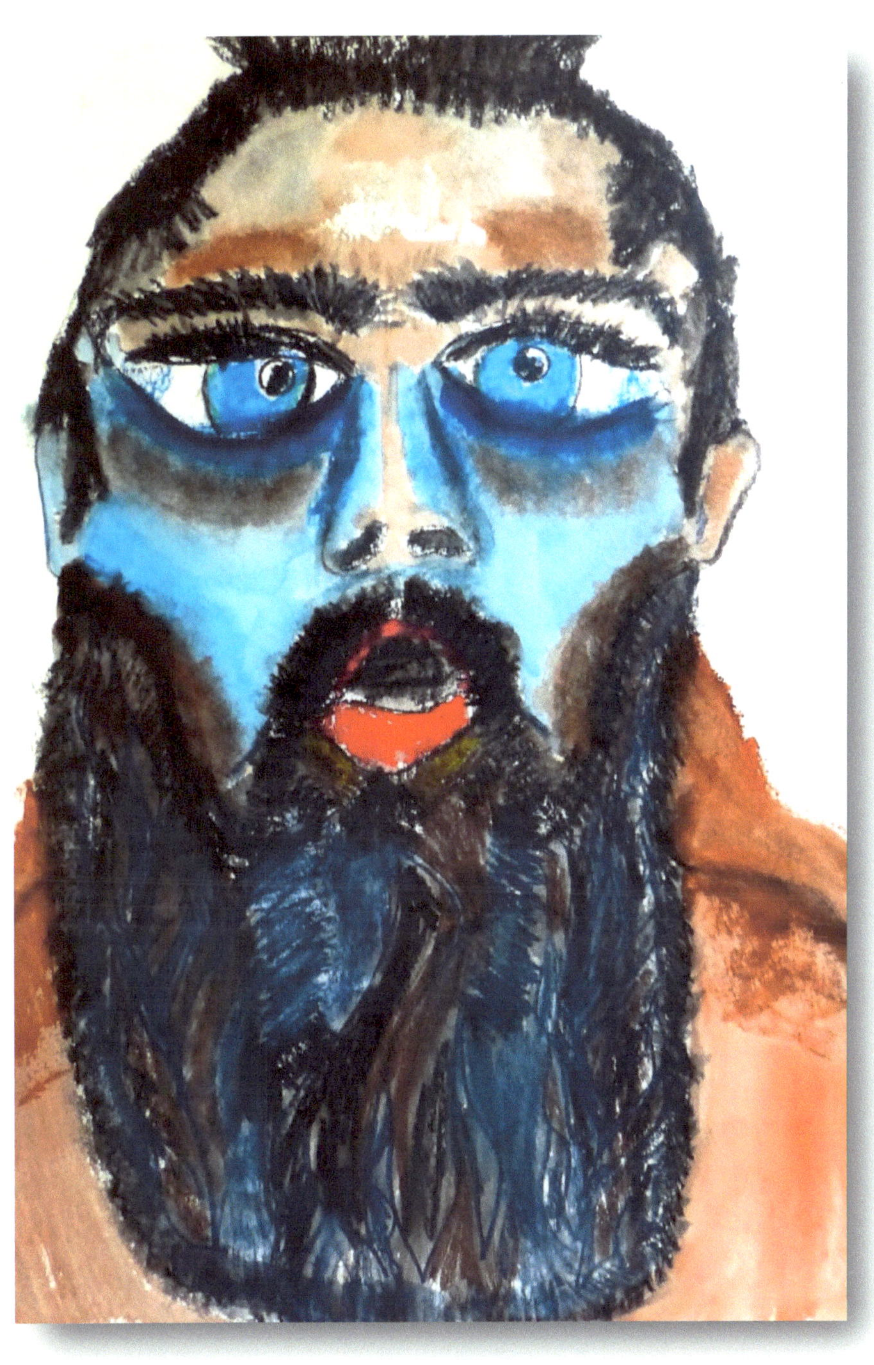

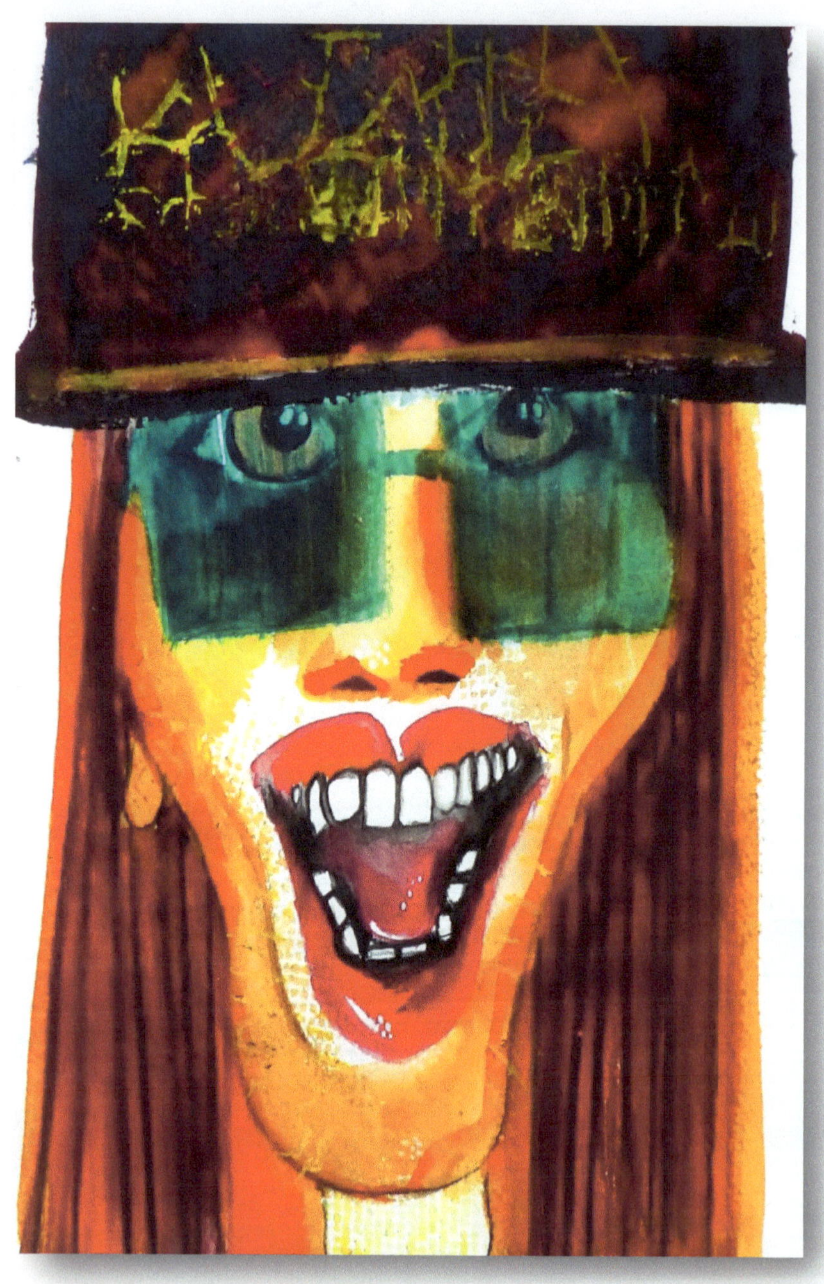

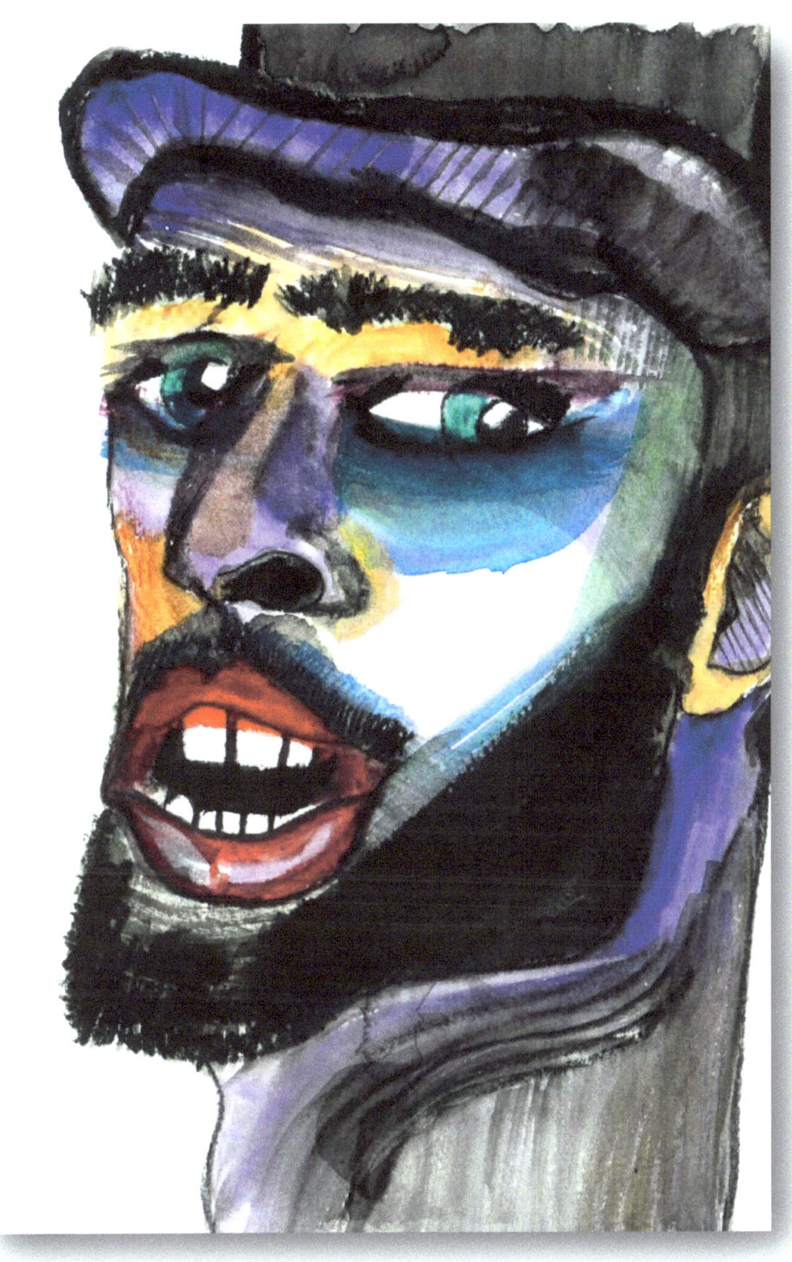

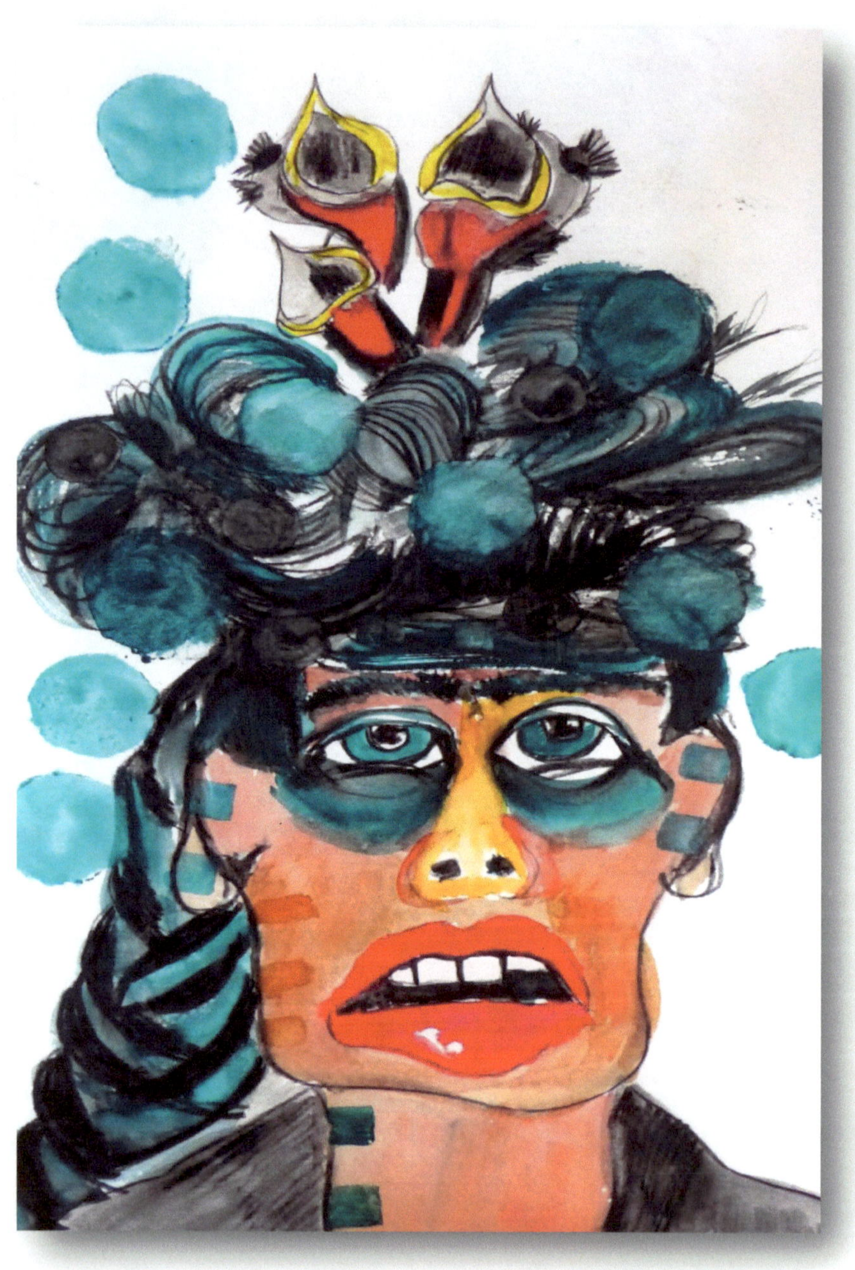

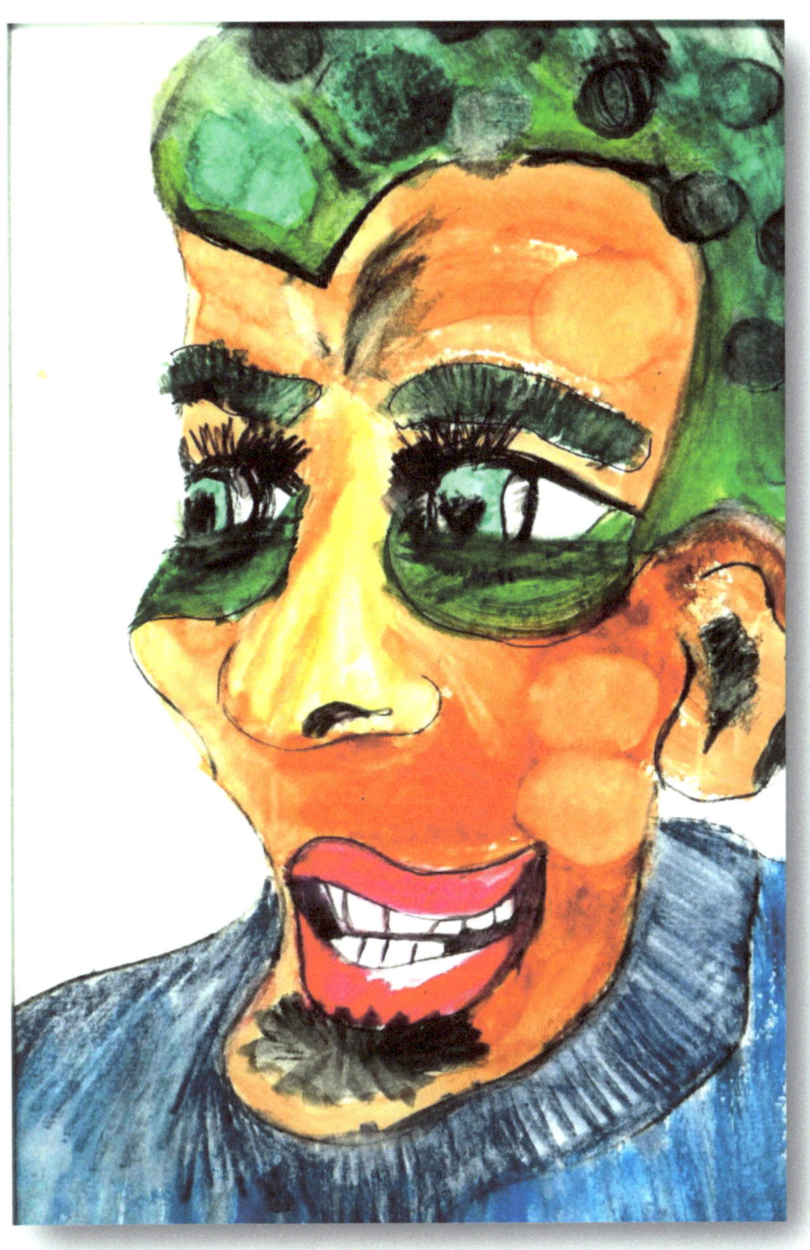

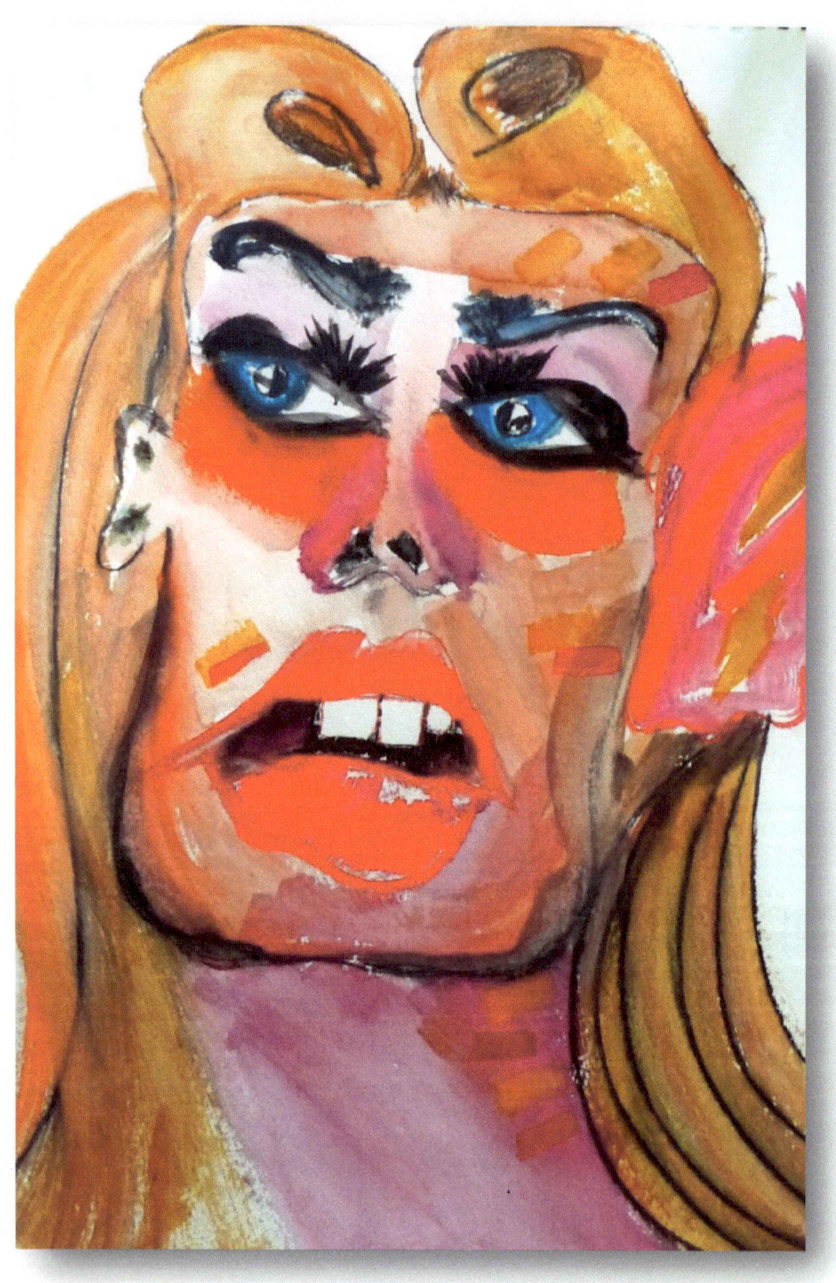

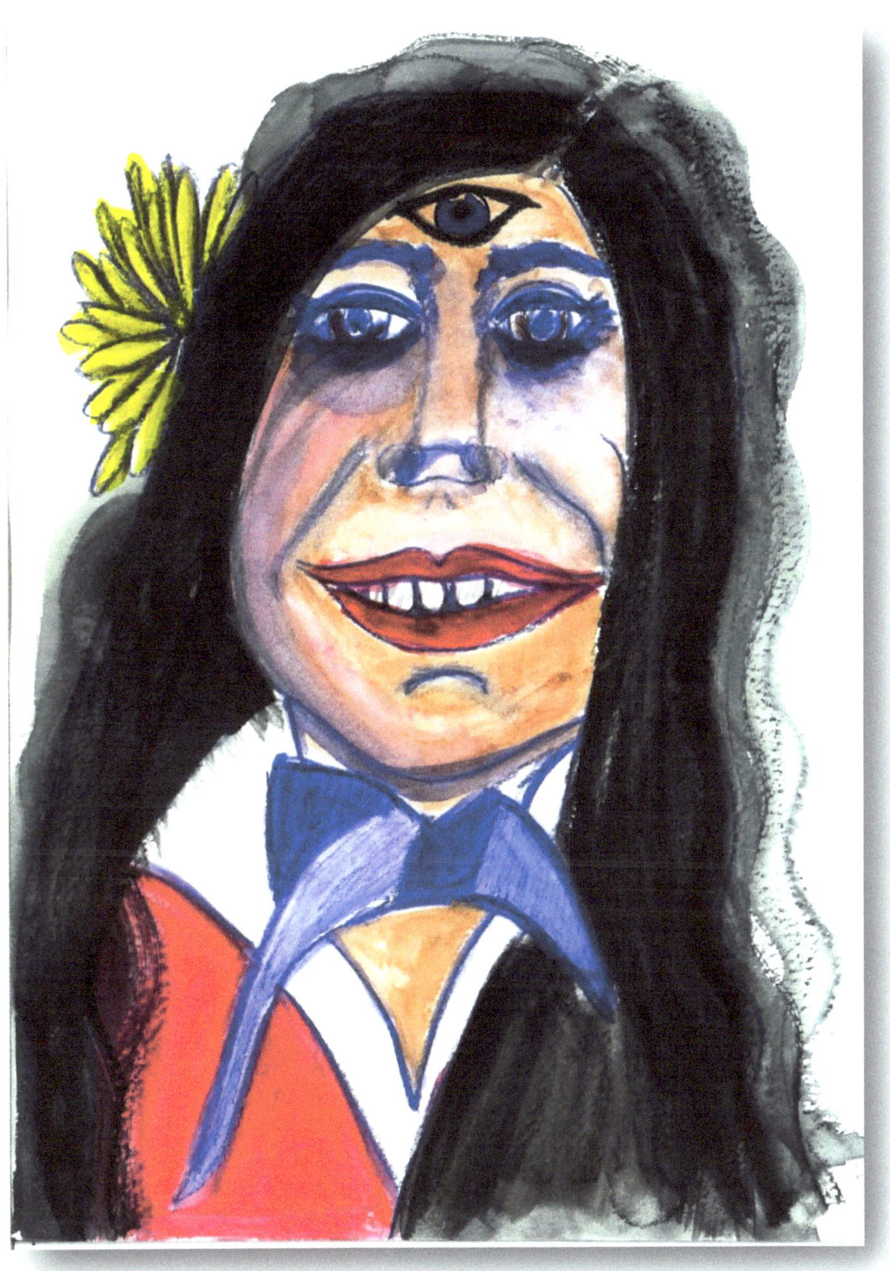

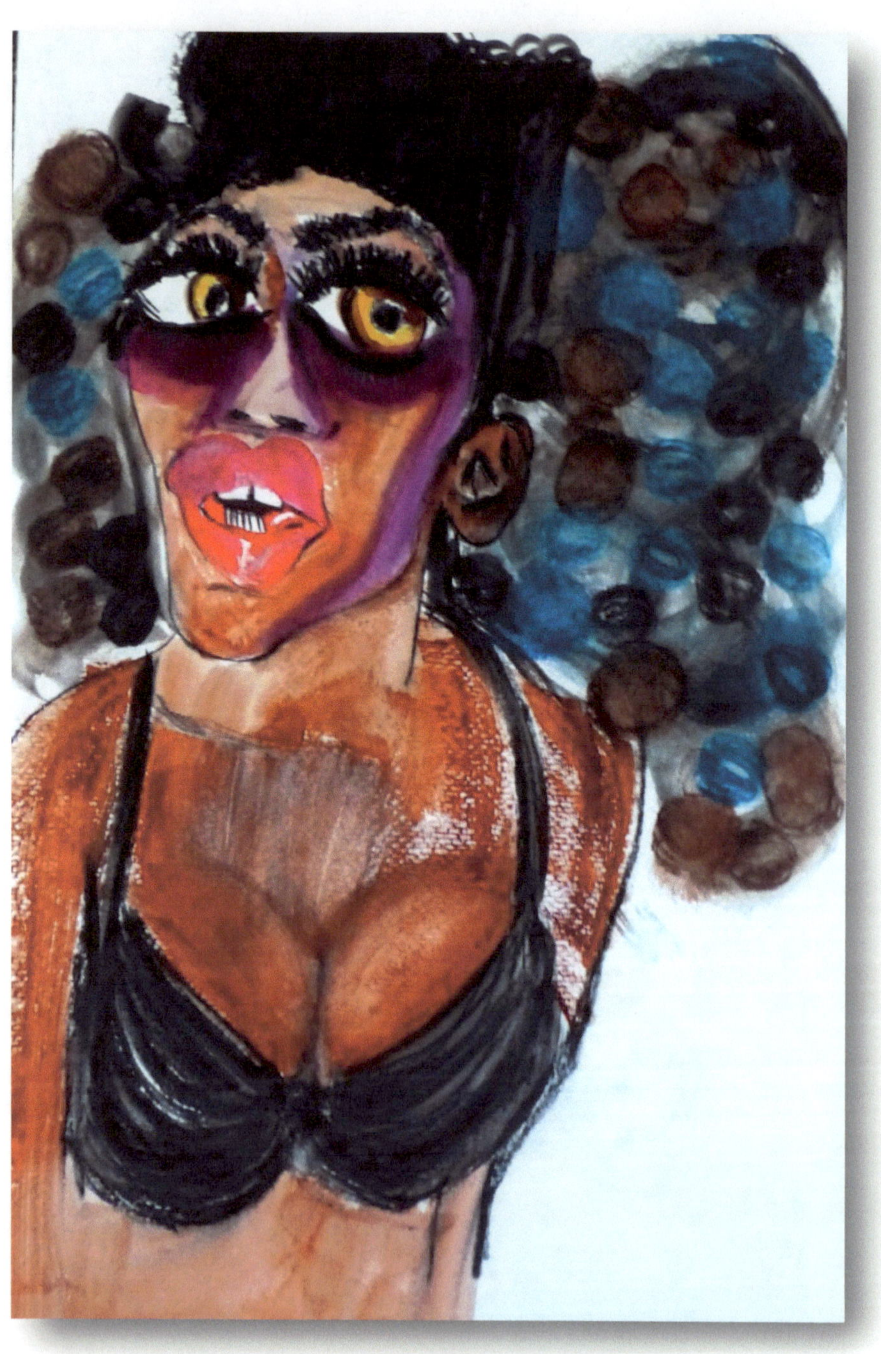

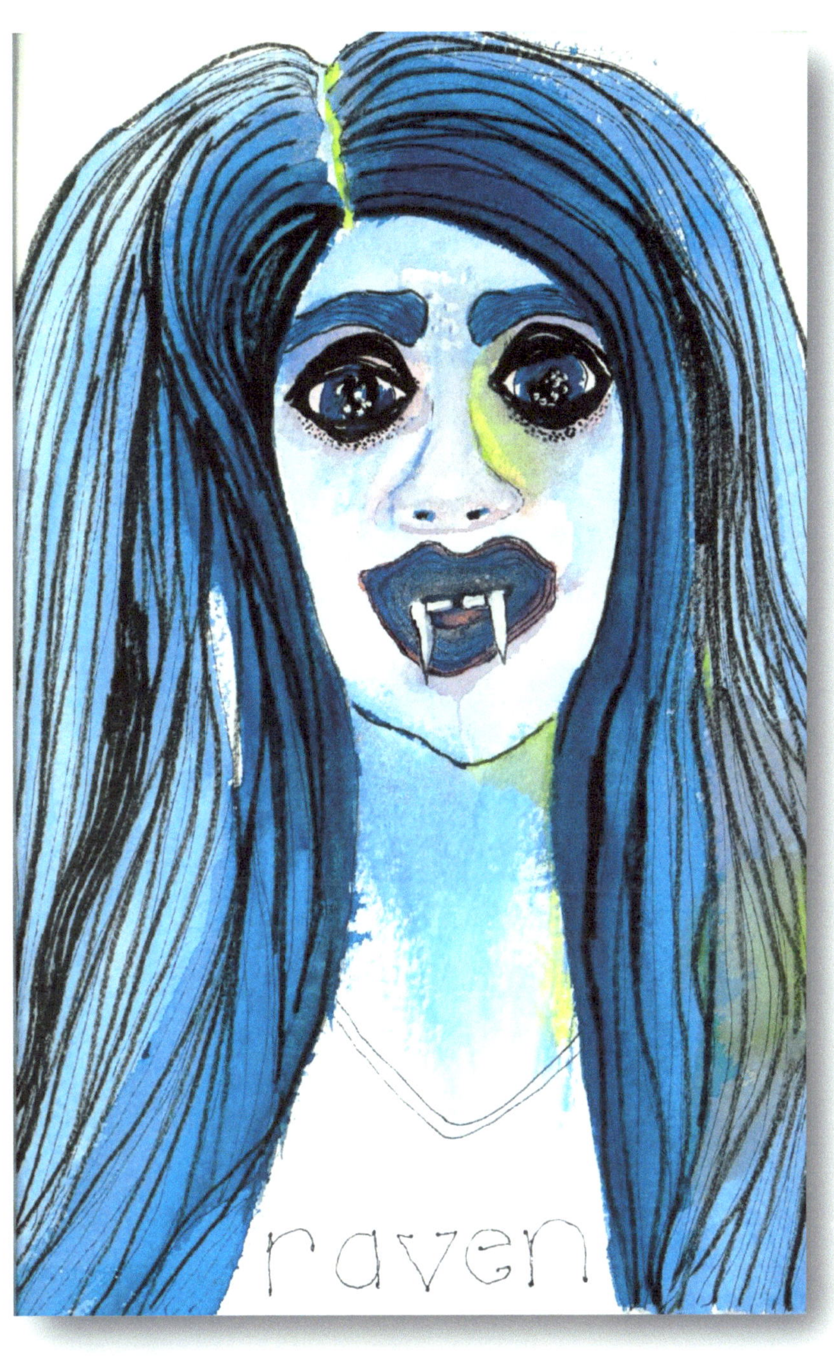
raven

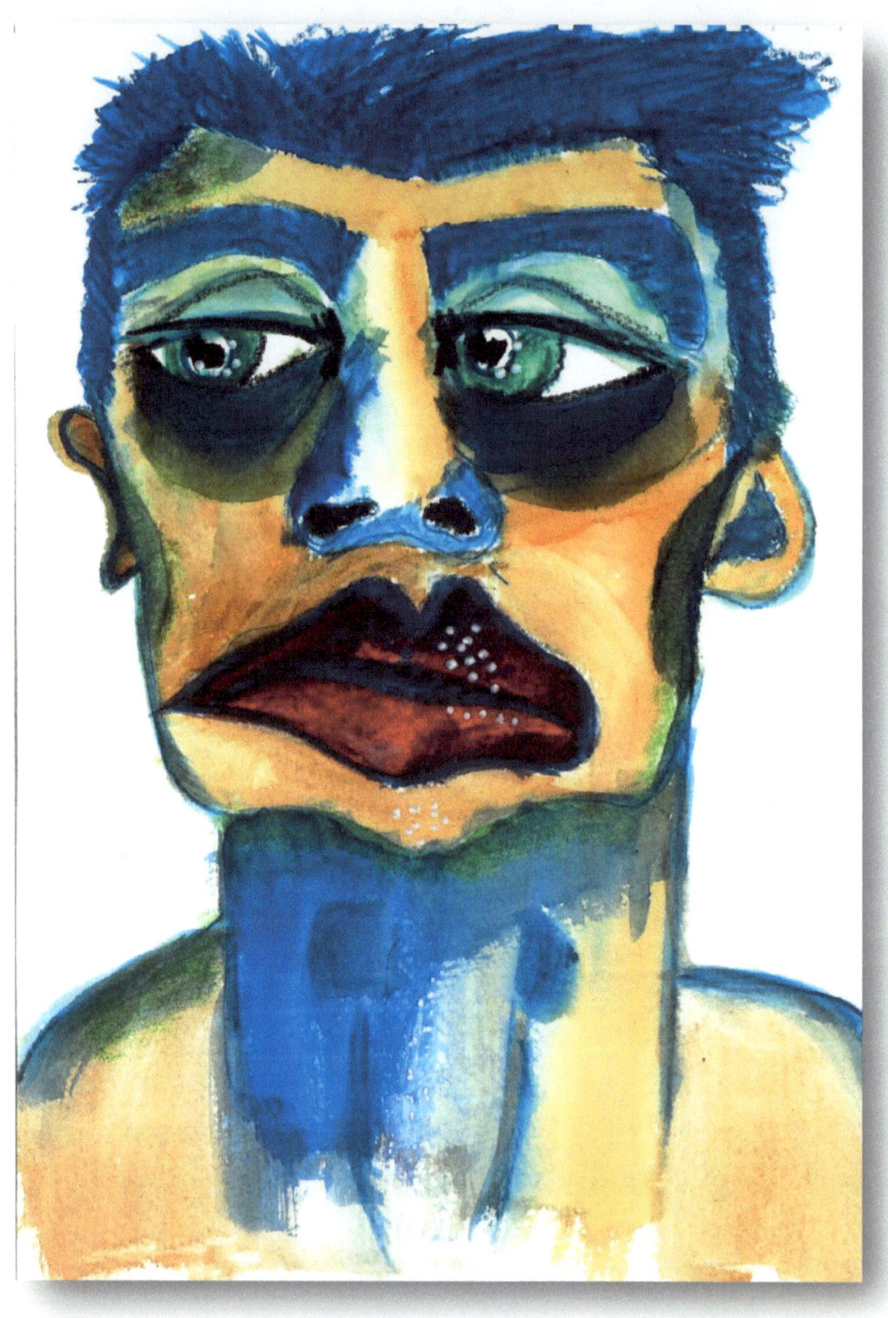

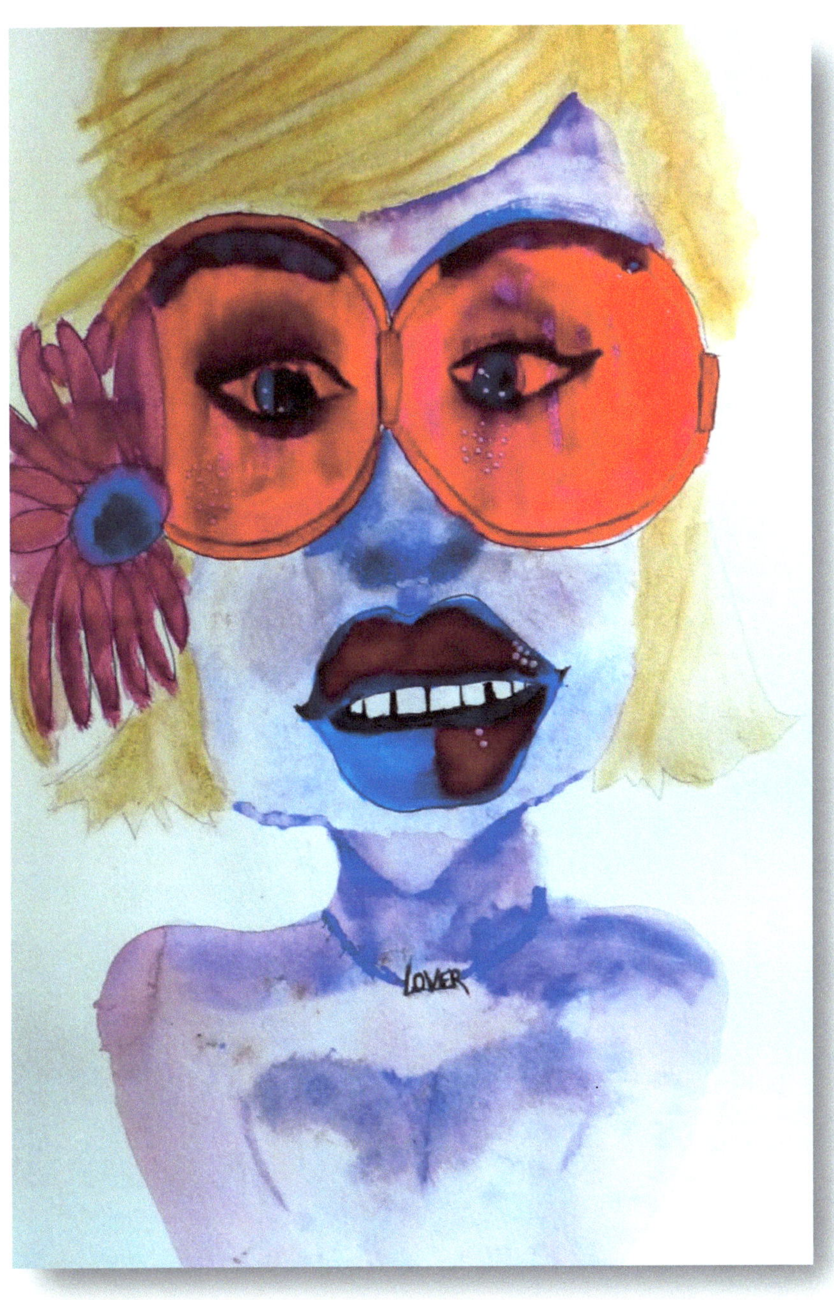
LOVER

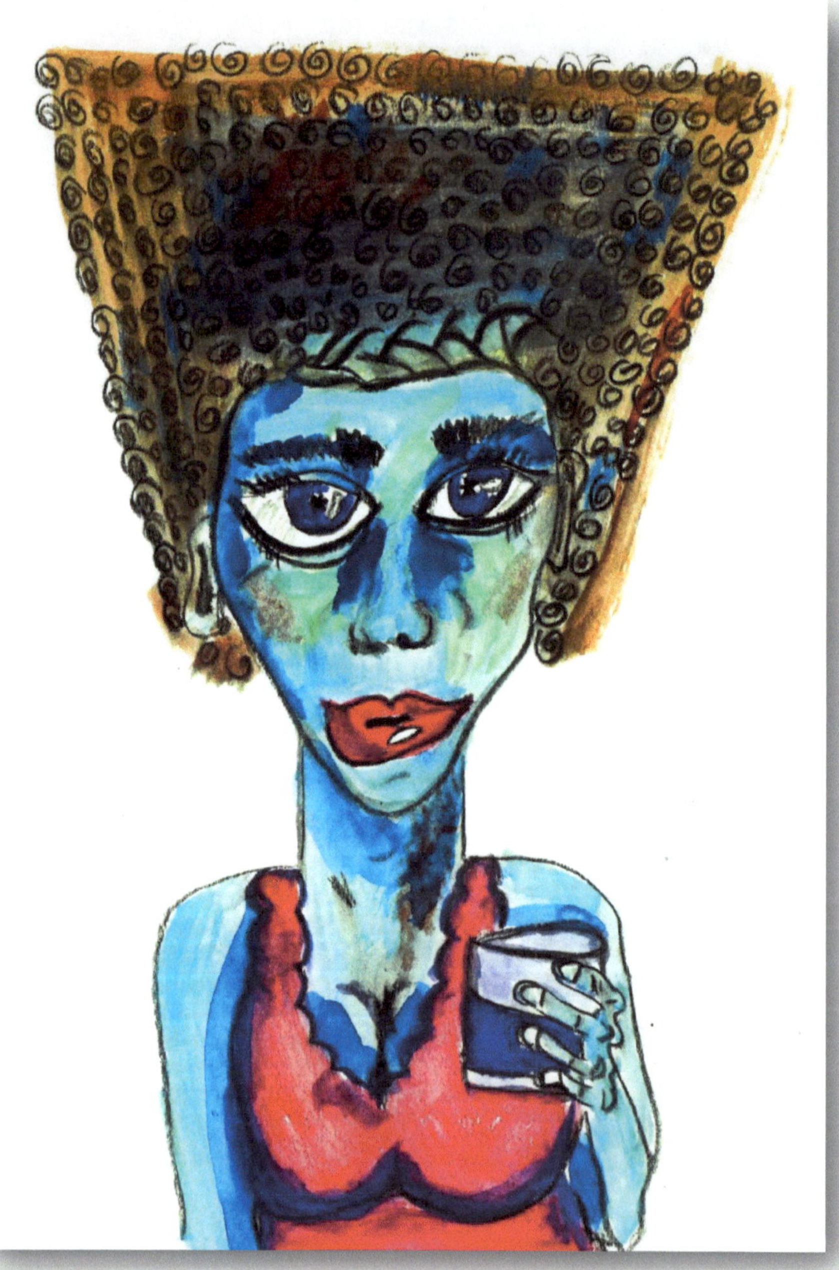

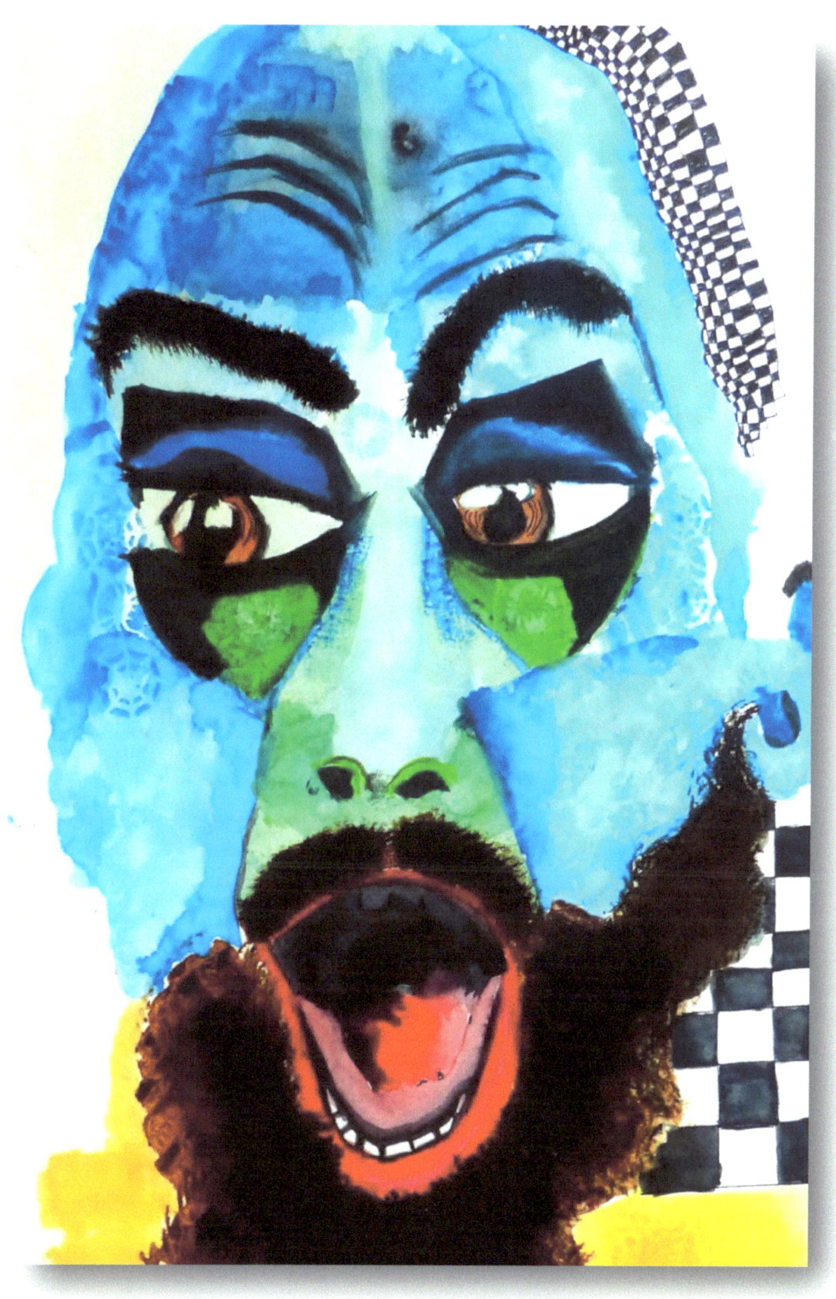

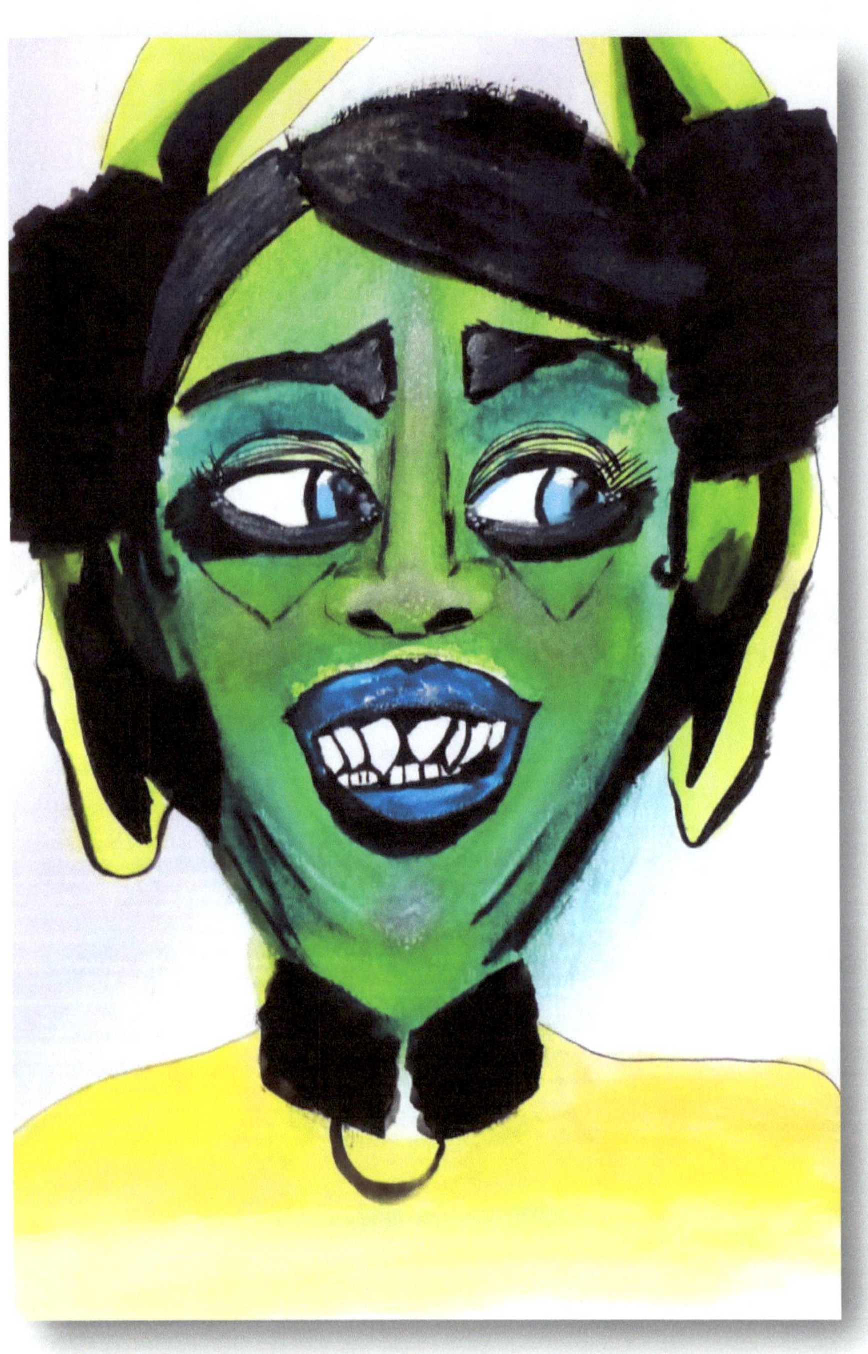

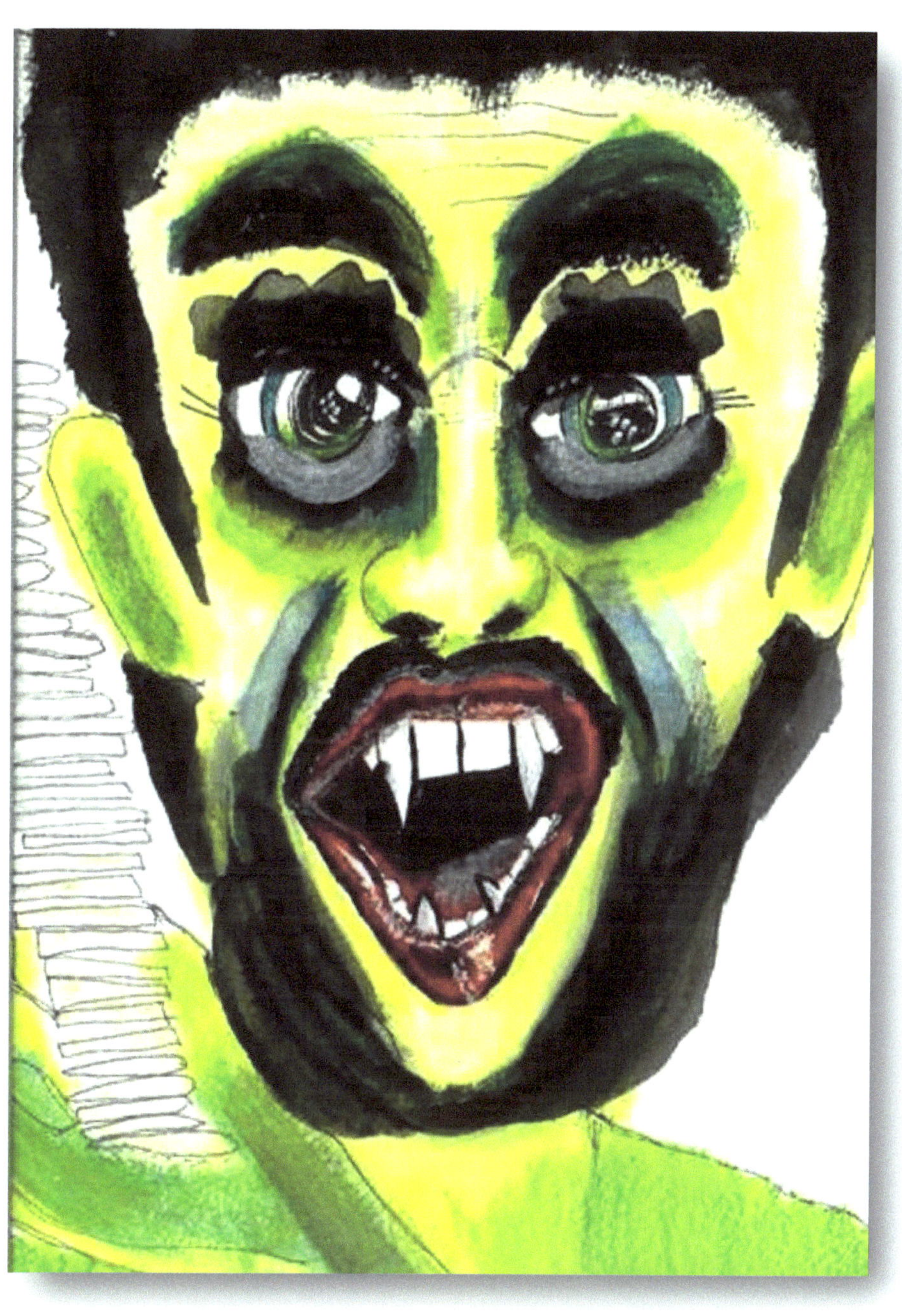

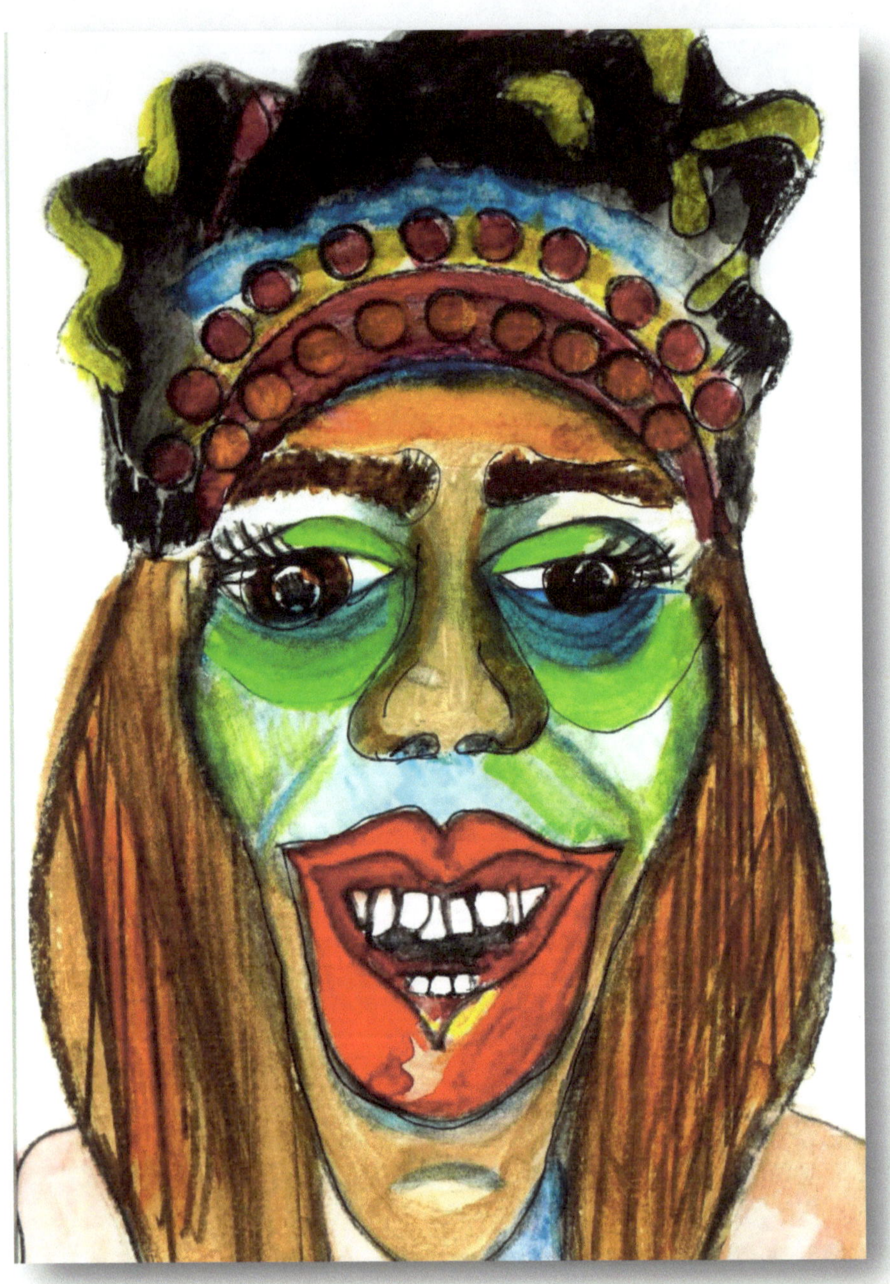

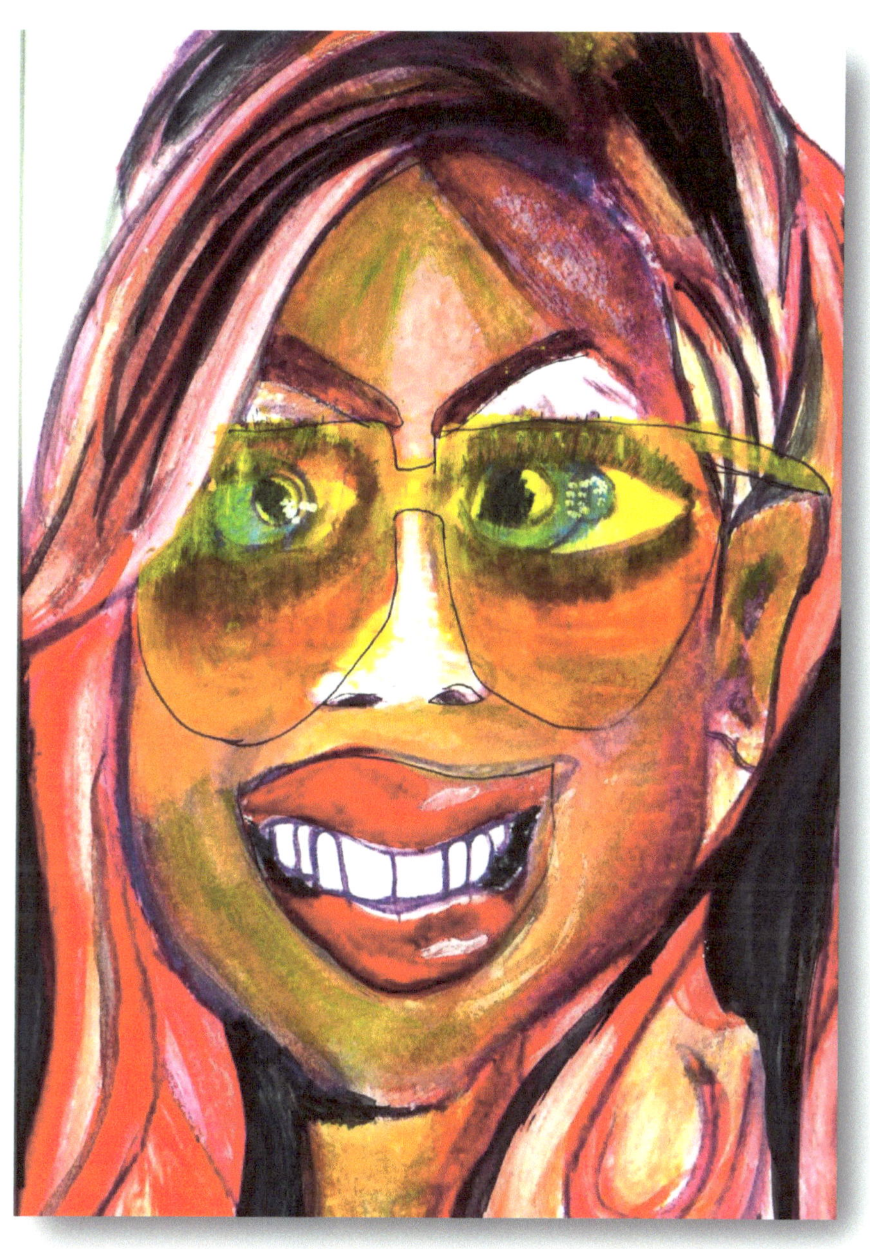

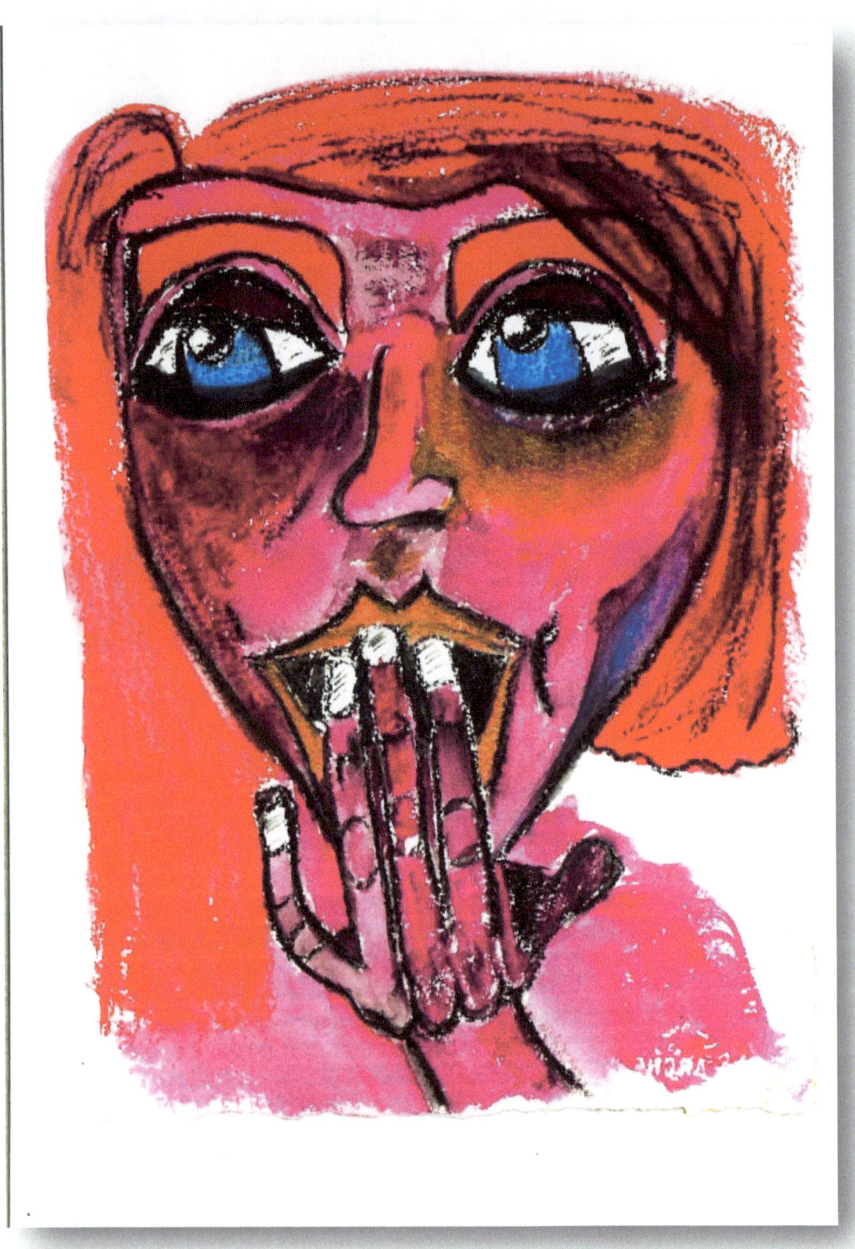

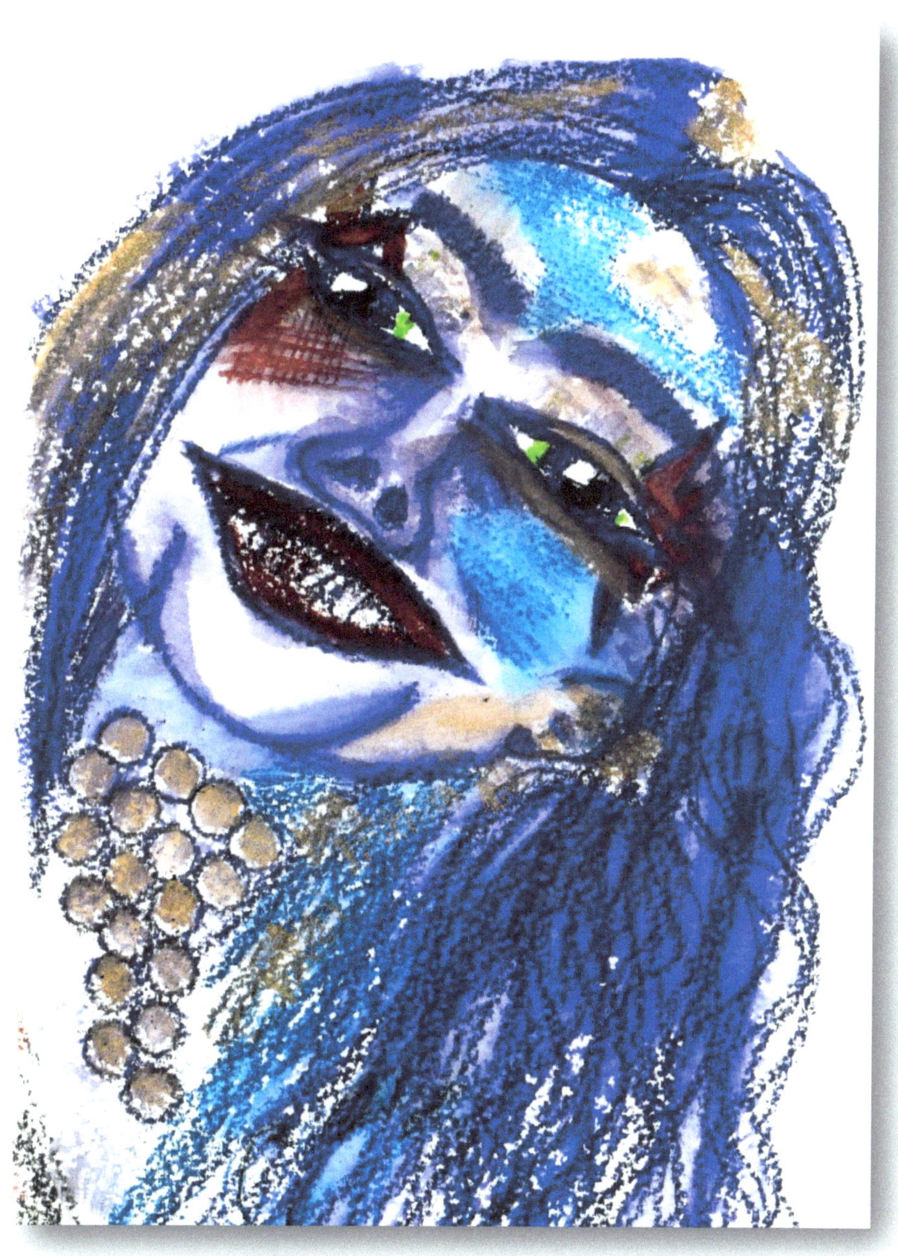

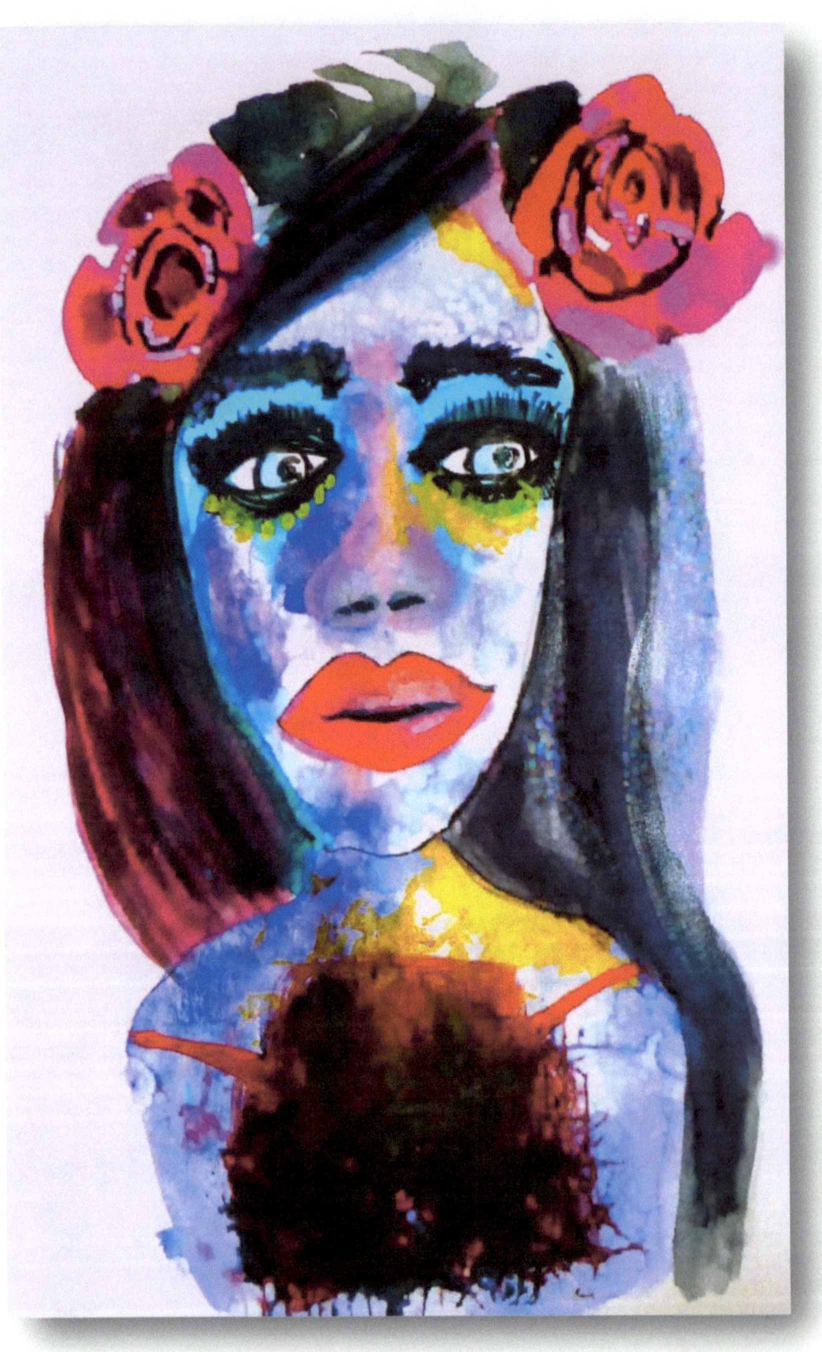

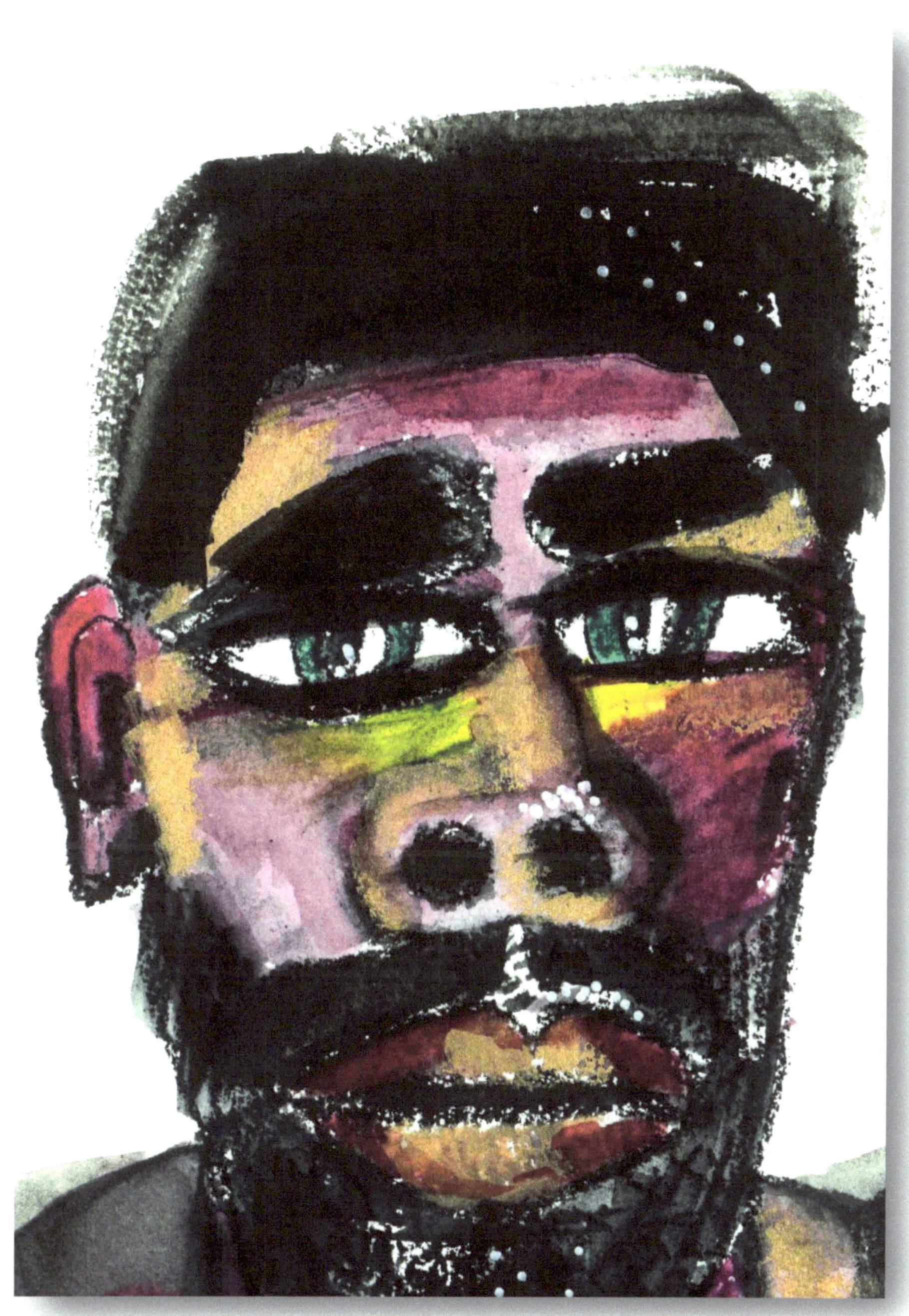

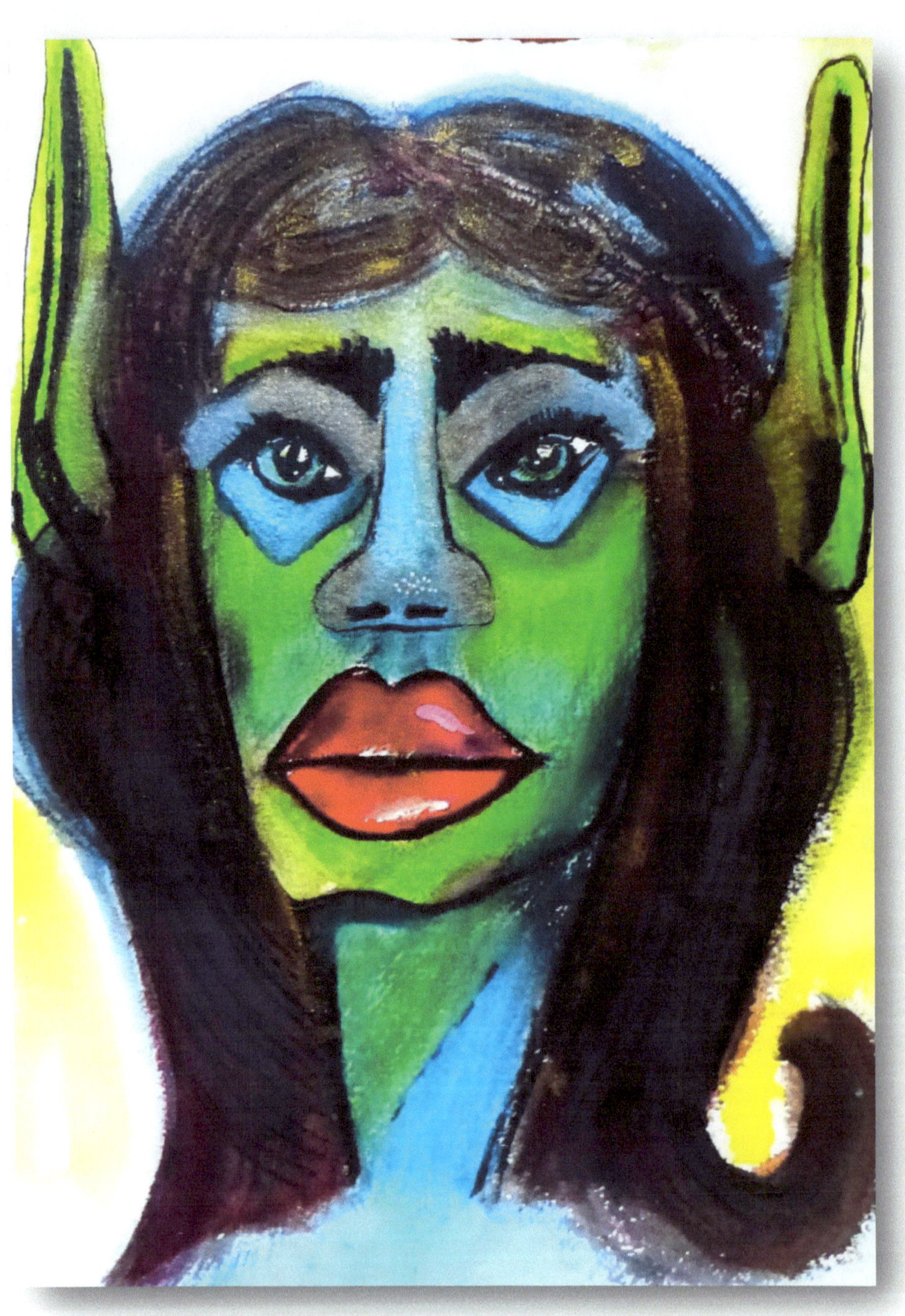

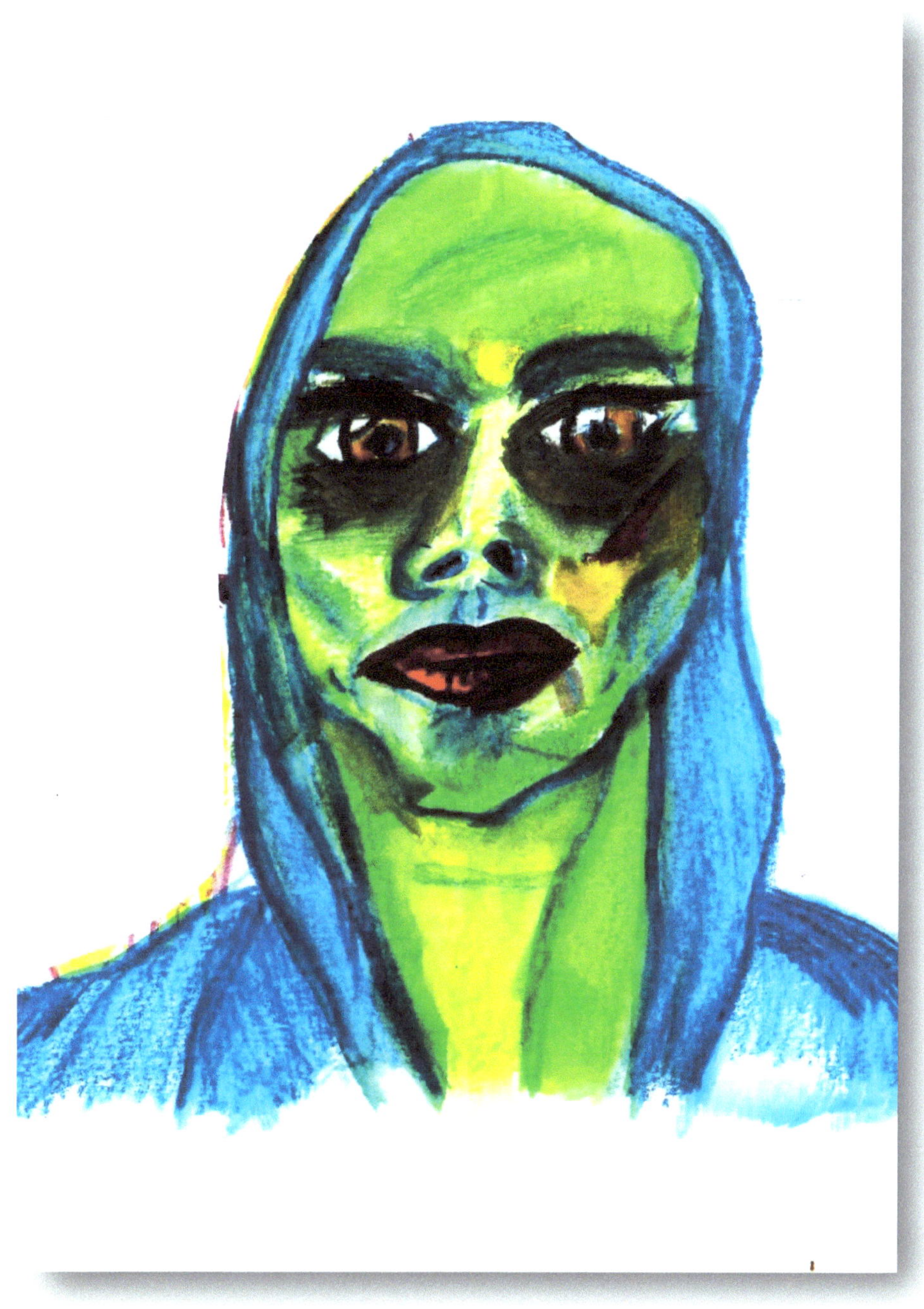

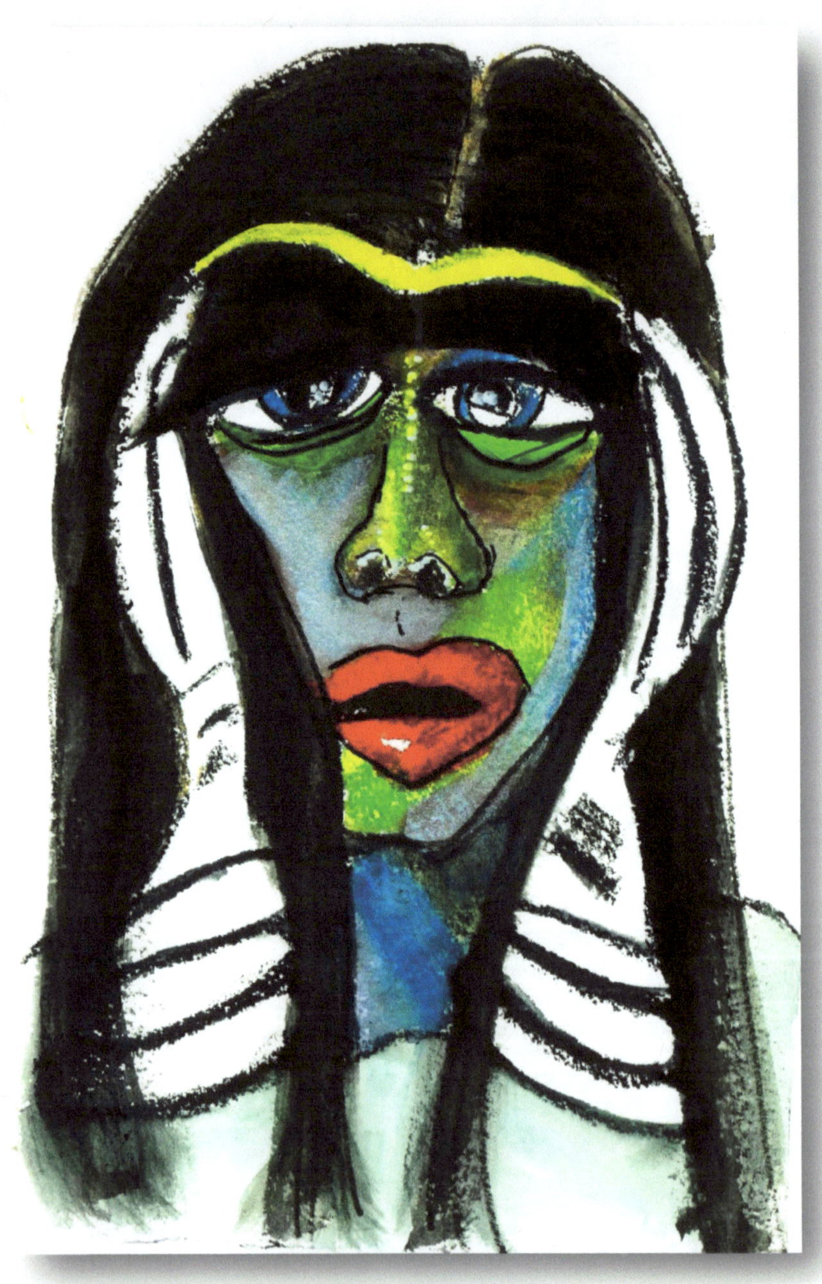

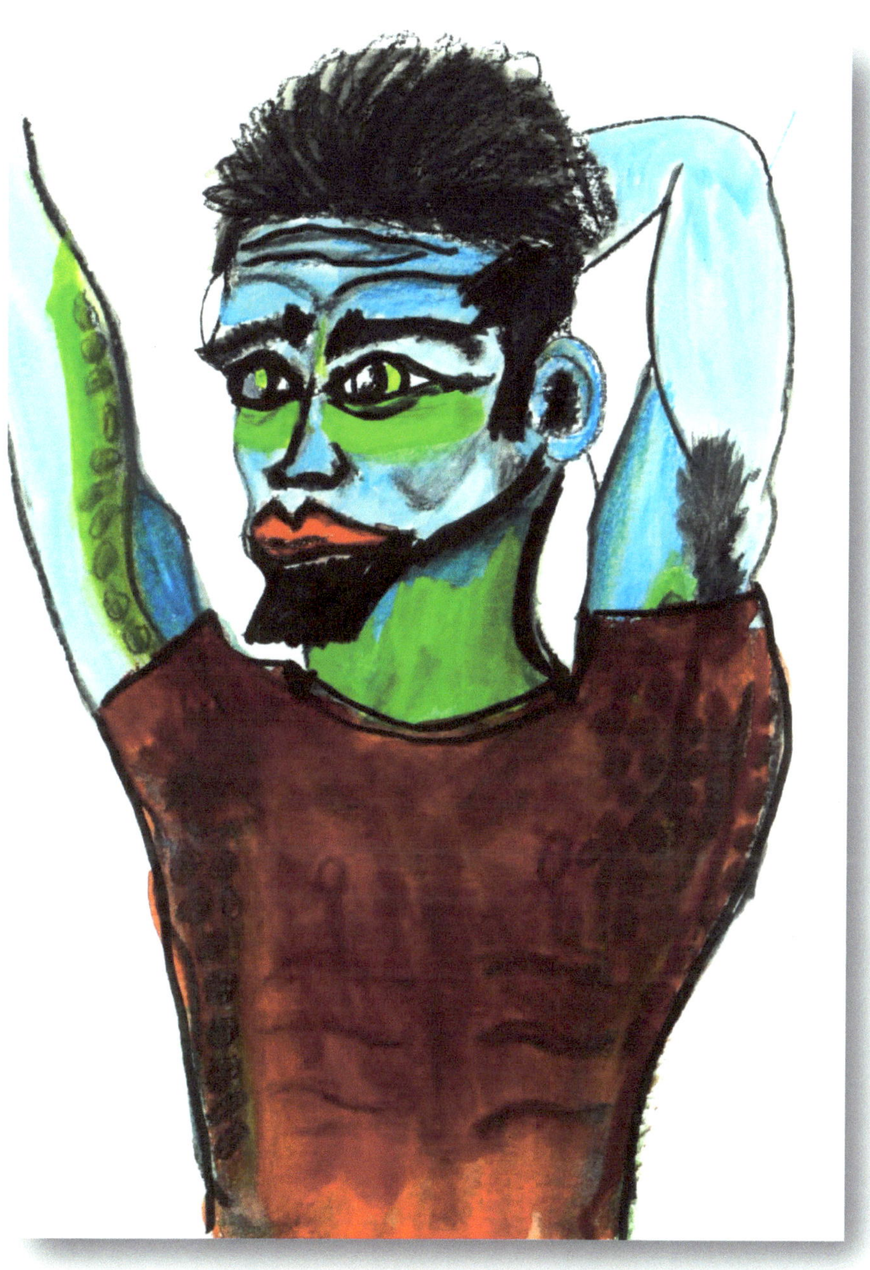

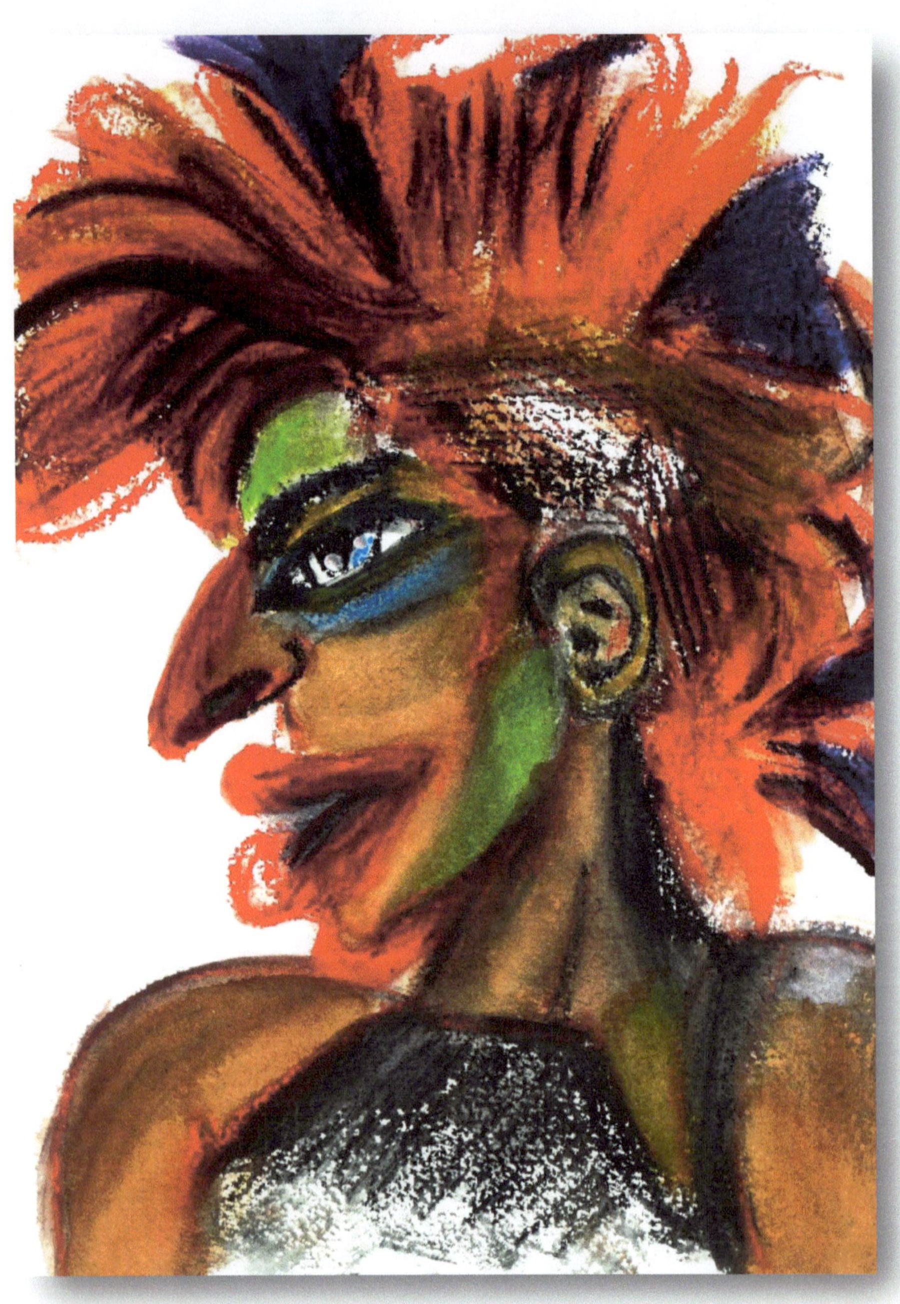

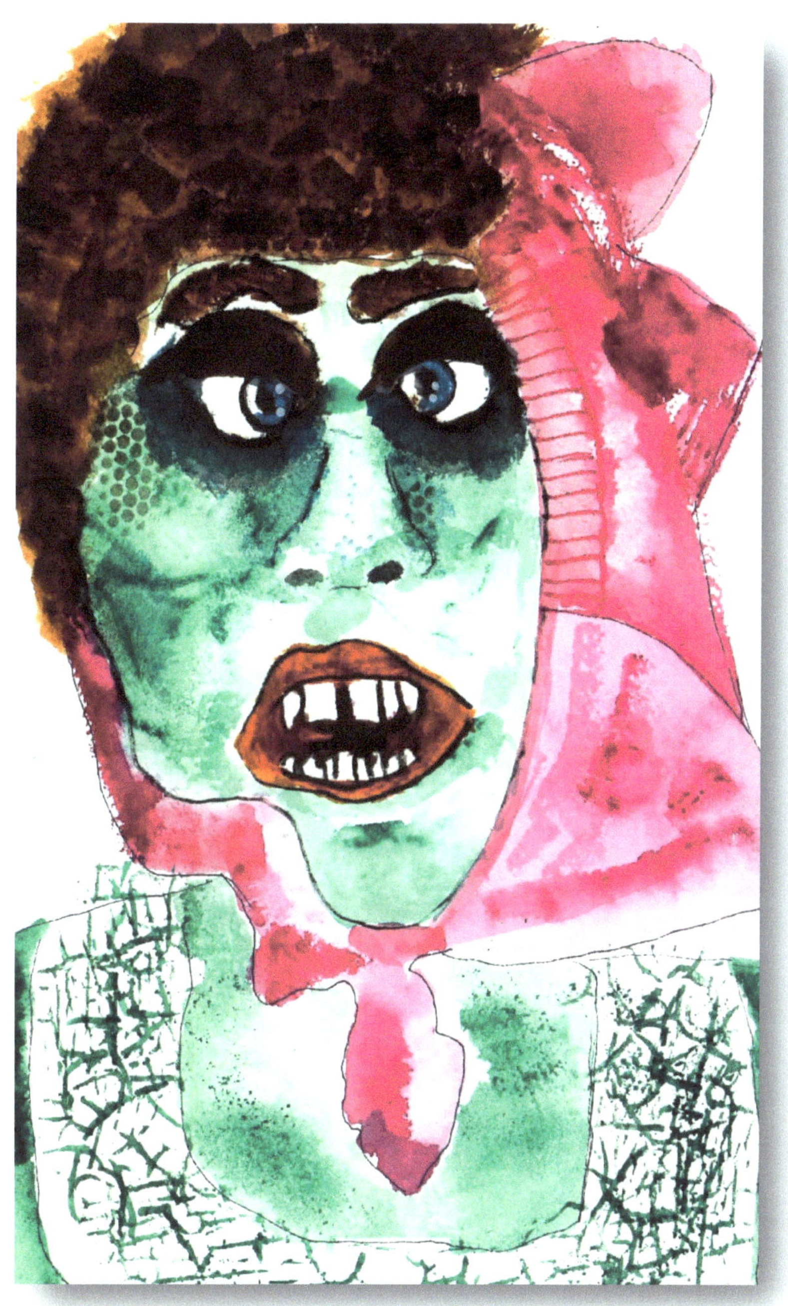

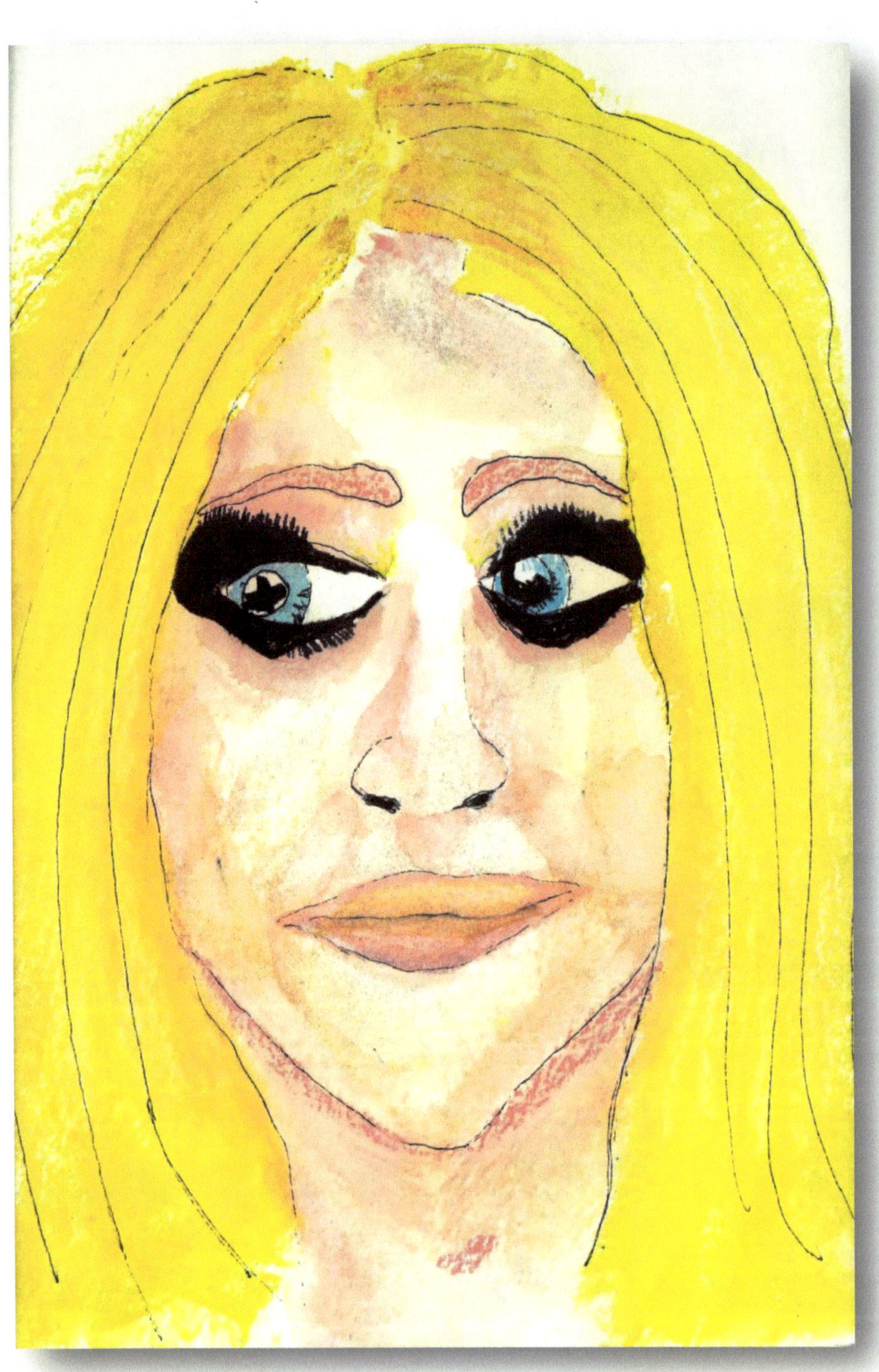

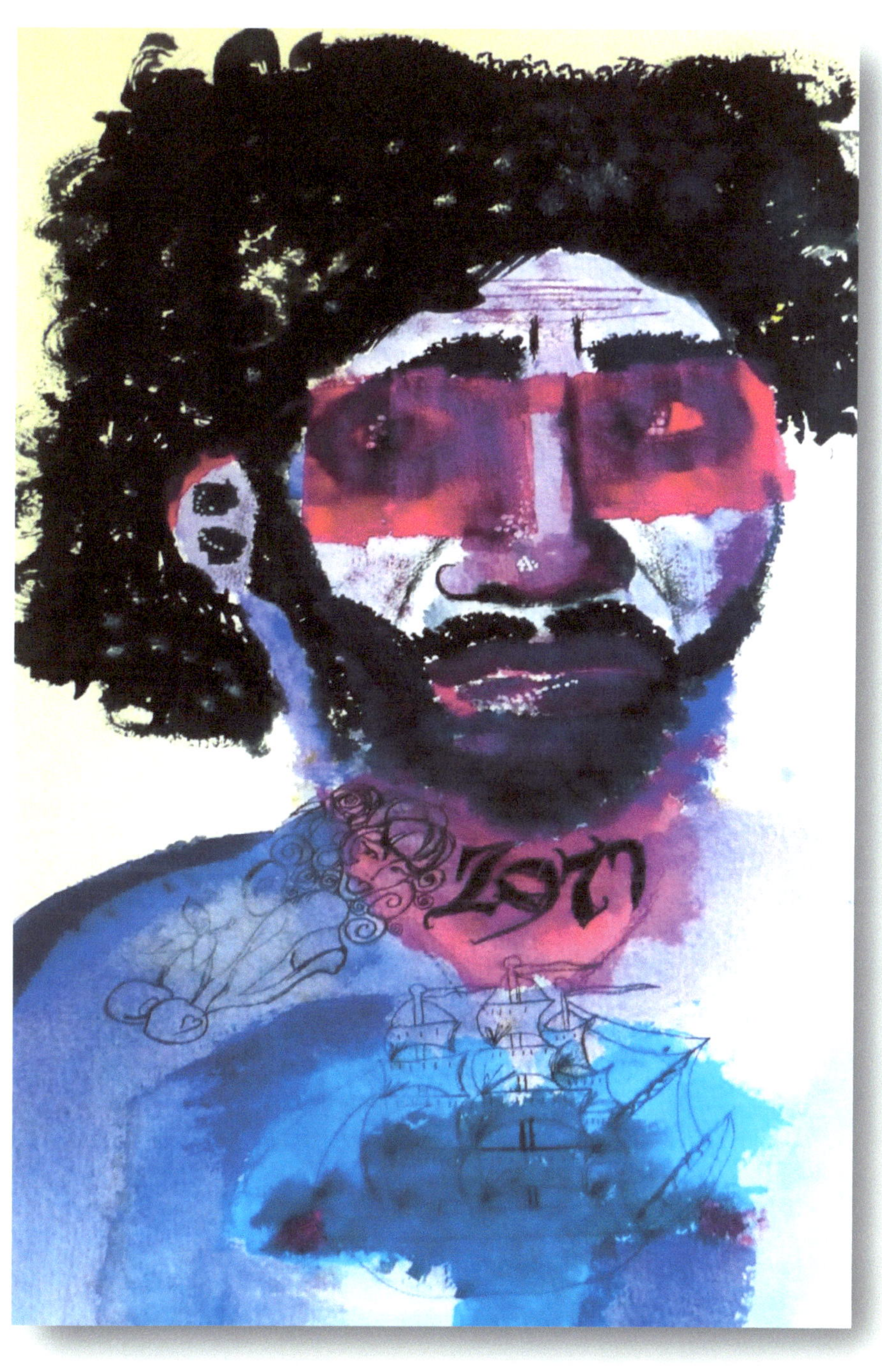

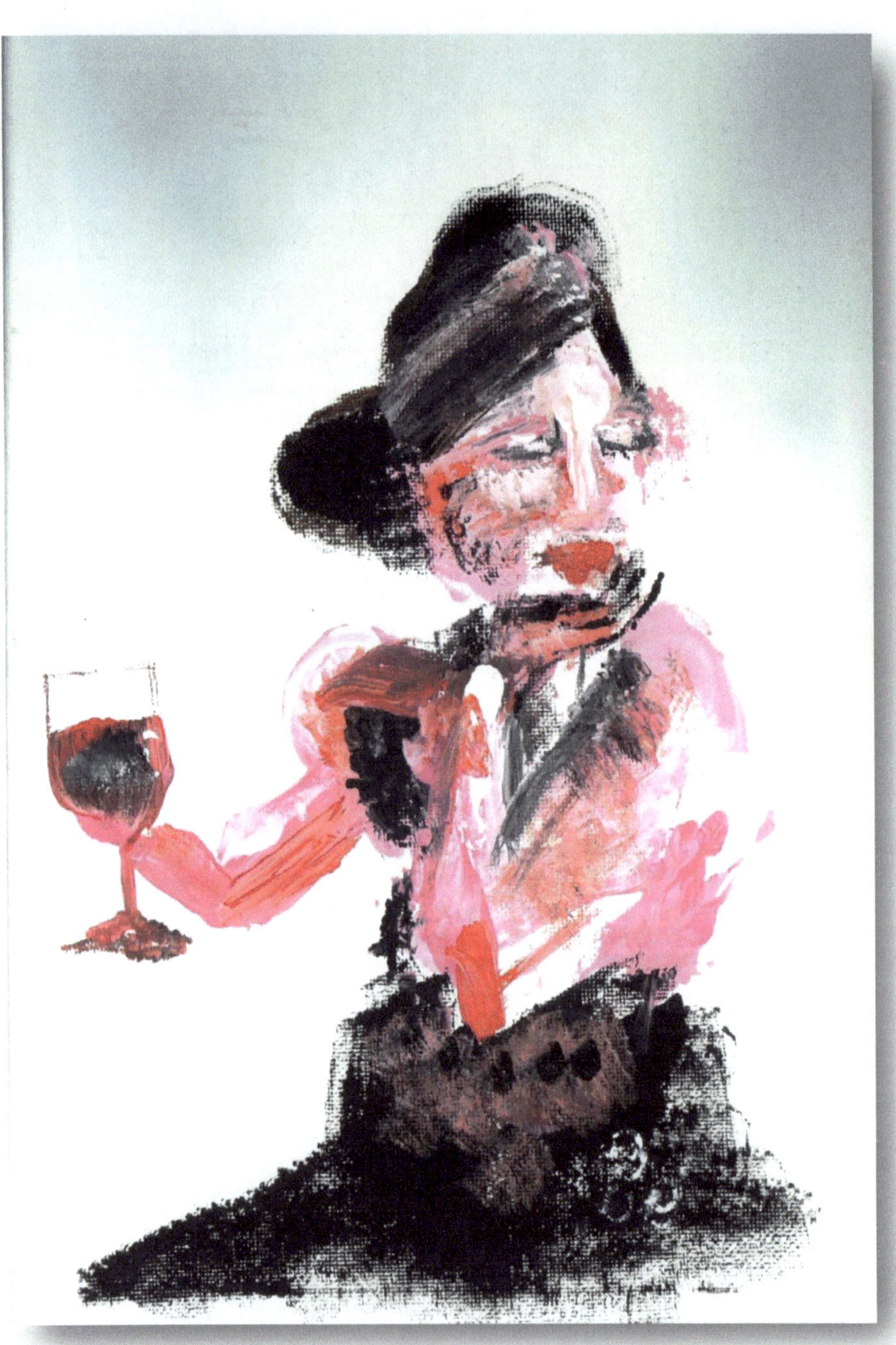

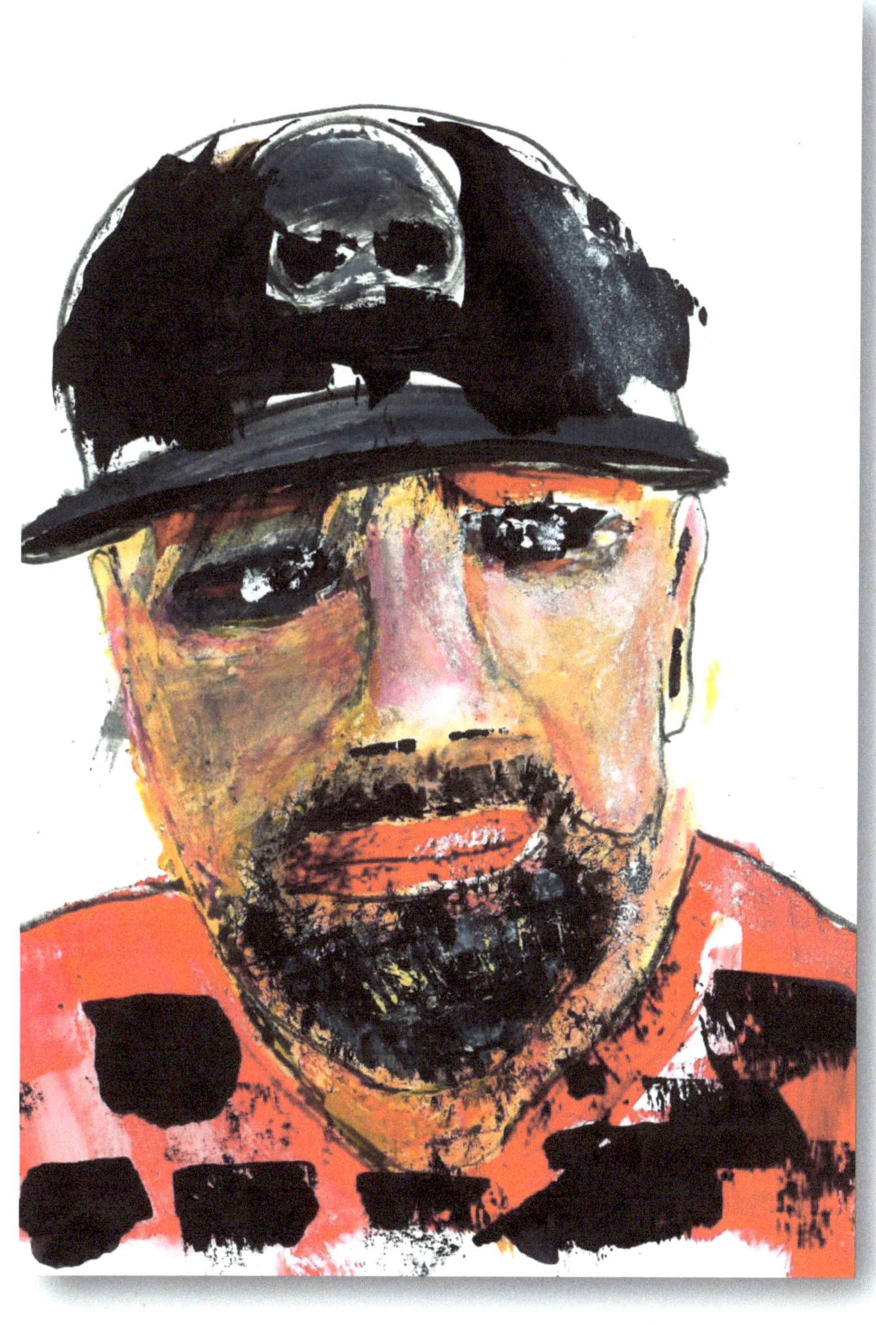

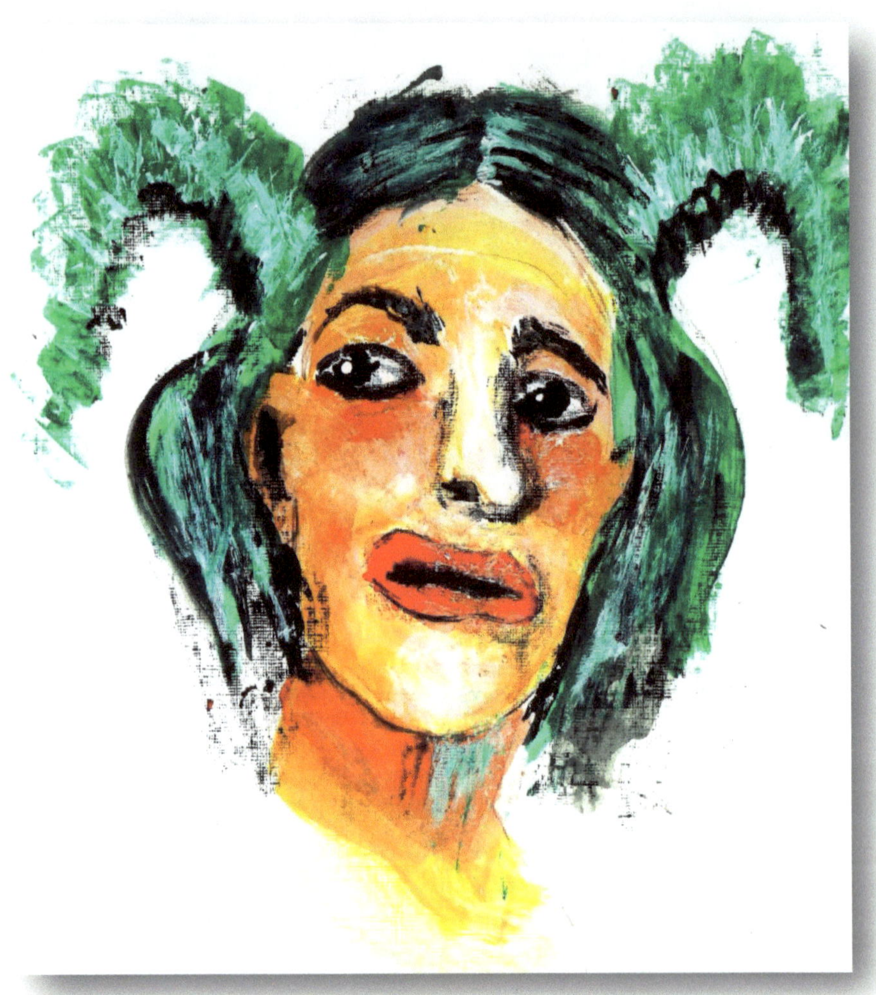

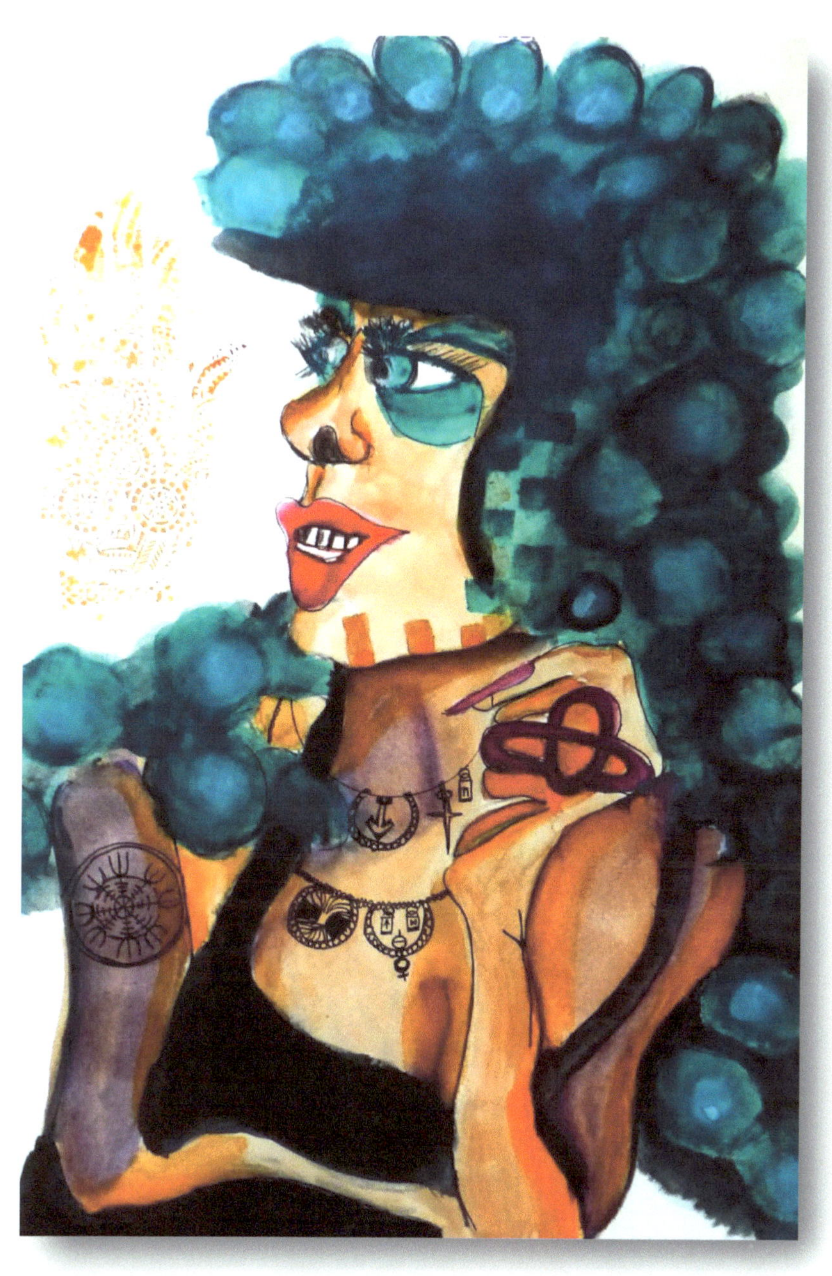

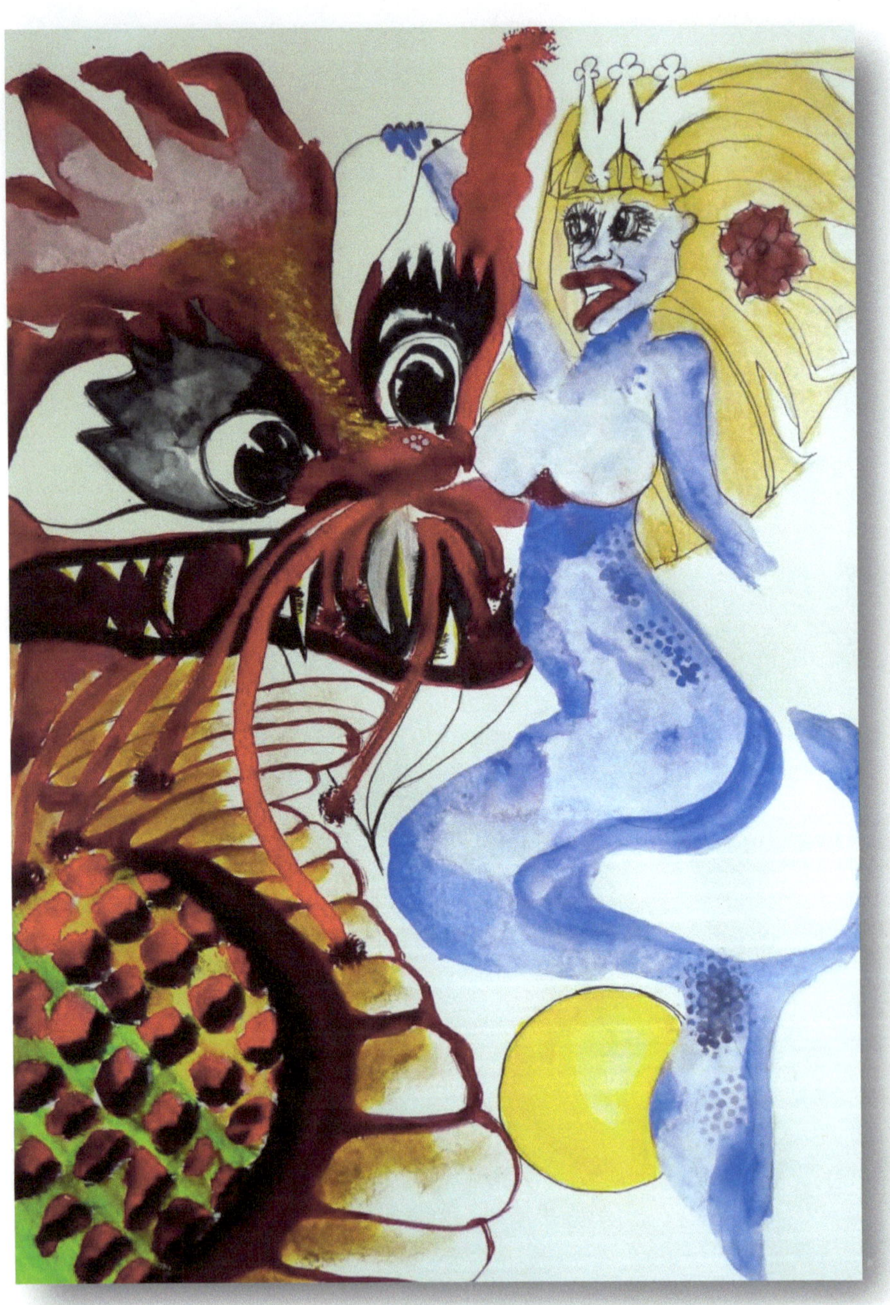

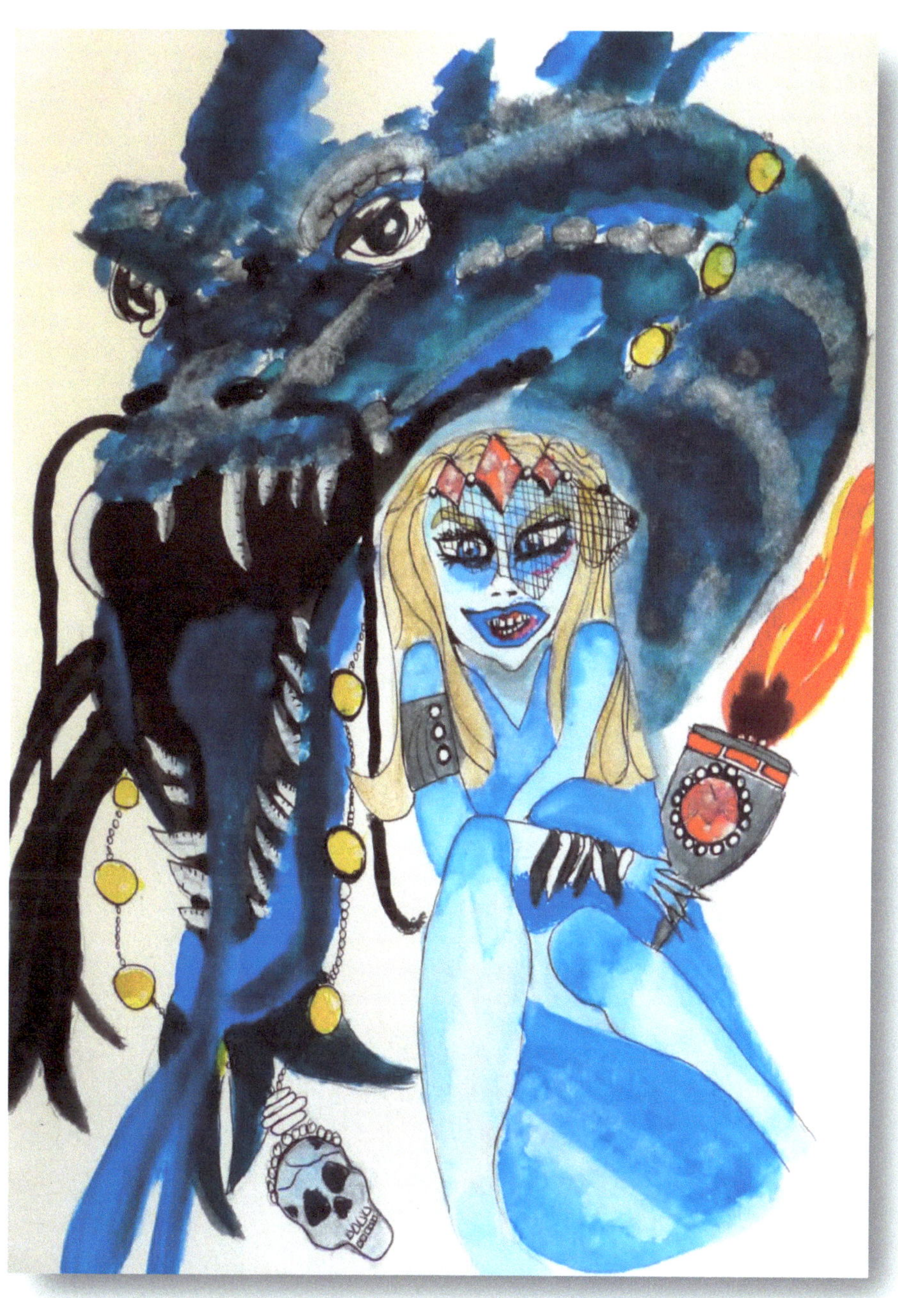

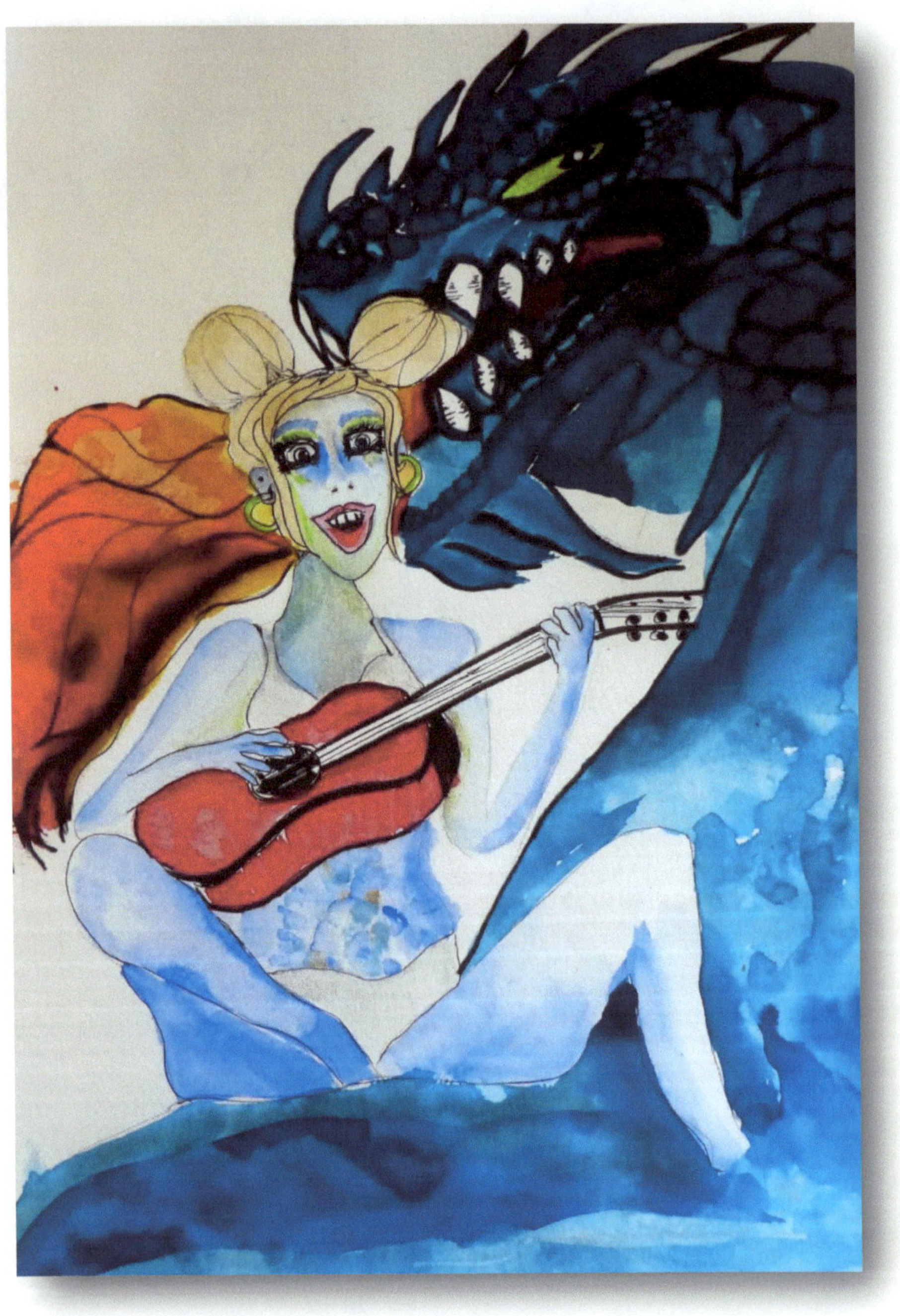

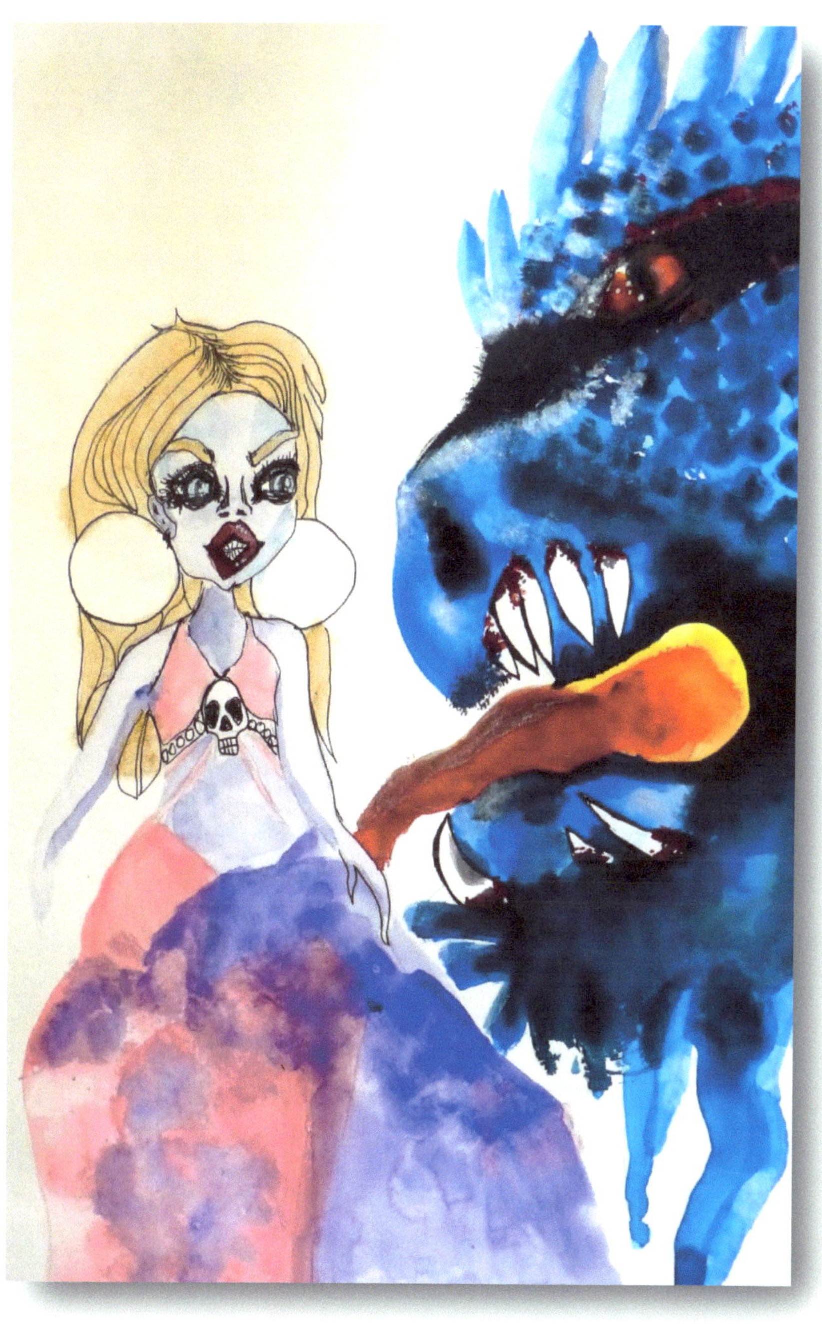

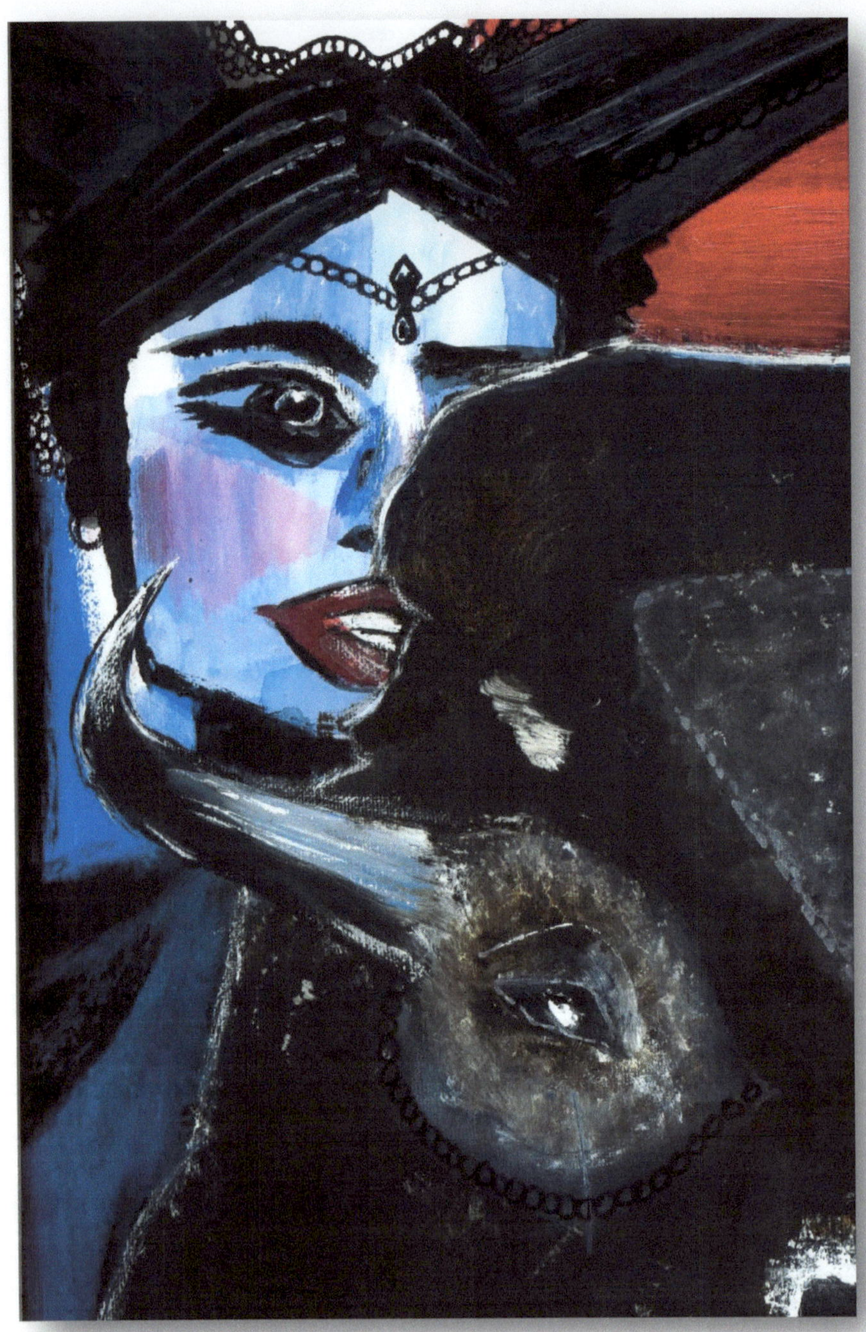

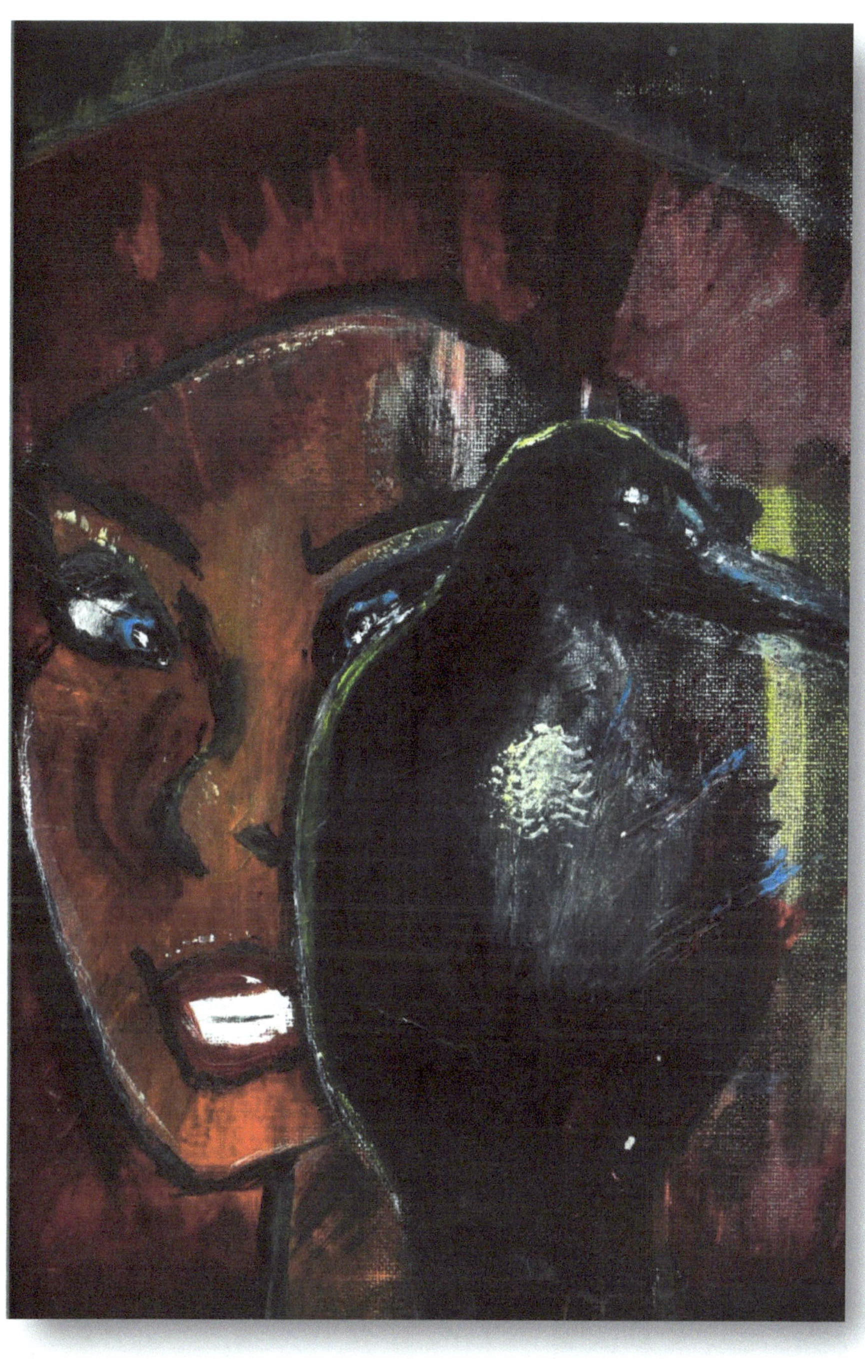

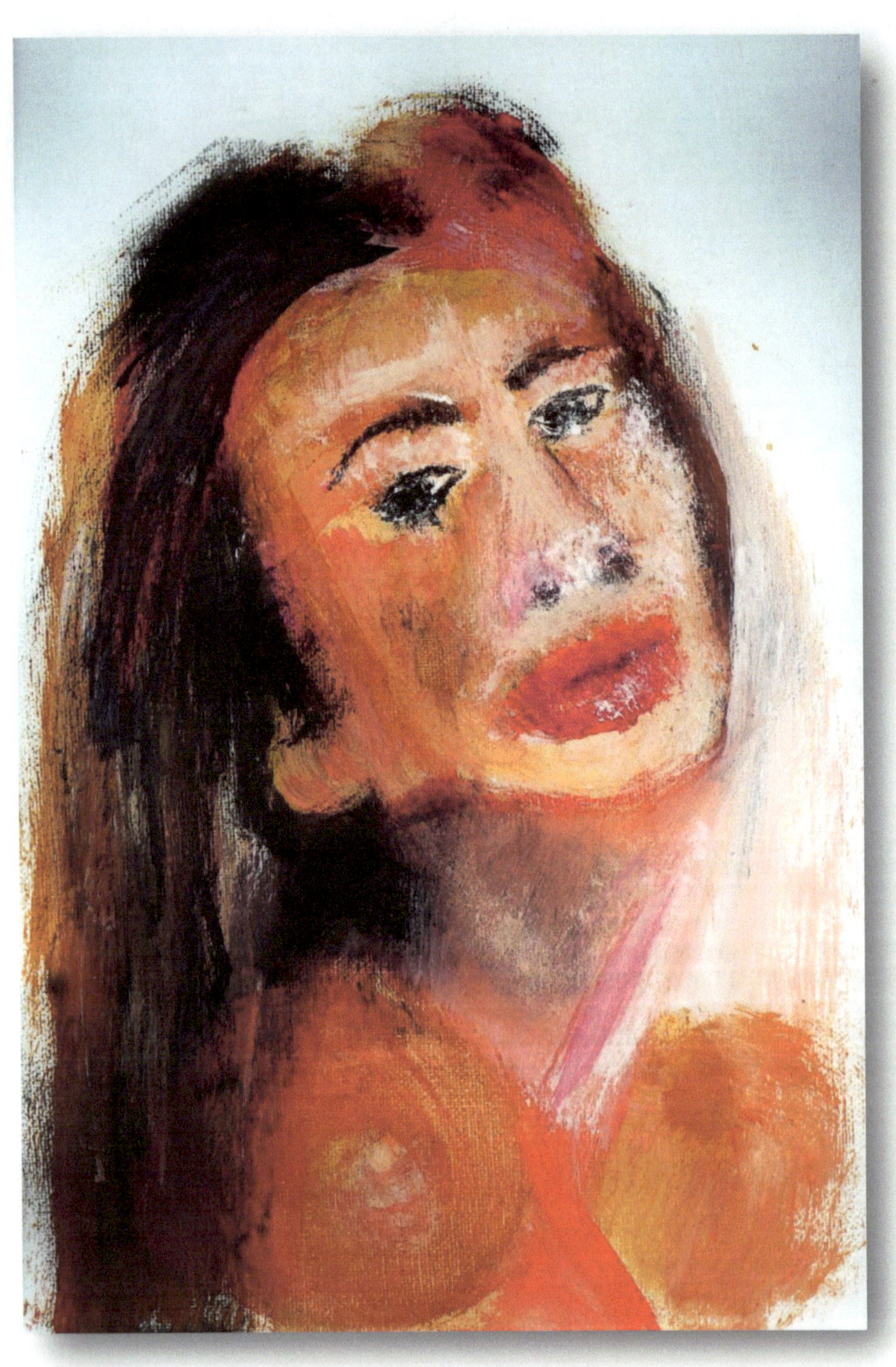

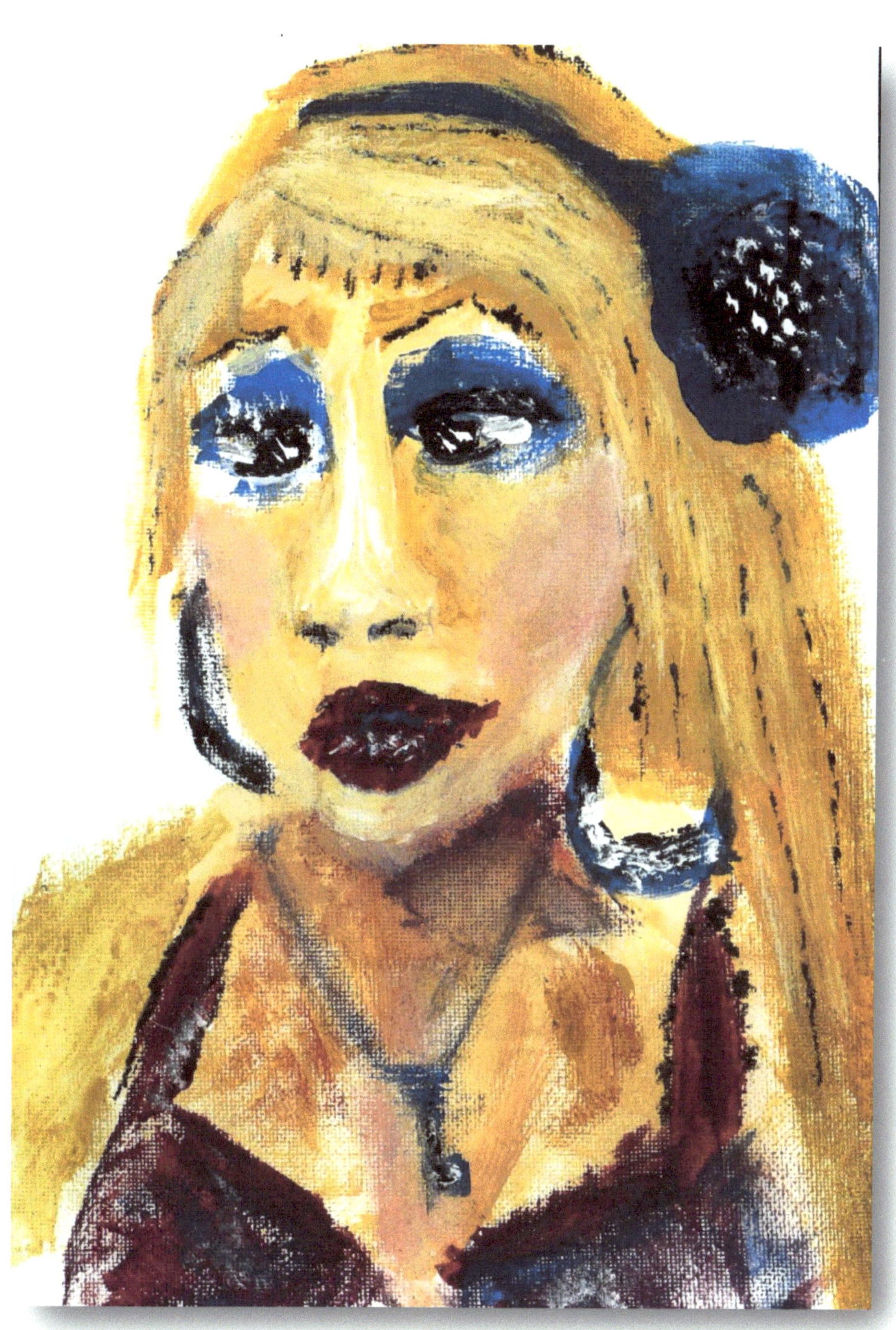

www.ingramcontent.com/pod-product-compliance
Lightning Source LLC
LaVergne TN
LVHW072029110826
845147LV00001BA/93

* 9 7 8 0 9 9 5 9 5 7 9 3 0 *